Building Basic Skills in Writing

Book 2

Building Basic Skills in Writing

Book 2

Contemporary Books, Inc.
Chicago

Library of Congress Cataloging in Publication Data
Main entry under title:

Building basic skills in writing.

   1. English language—Grammar—1950-
   2. Basic education   I. Contemporary Books, inc.
PE1112.B74   808′.042   81-802
ISBN 0-8092-5841-2 (pbk.)   AACR2

Published by Contemporary Books, Inc.
180 North Michigan Avenue, Chicago, Illinois 60601
Manufactured in the United States of America
Library of Congress Catalog Card Number: 81-802
International Standard Book Number: 0-8092-5841-2

Published simultaneously in Canada by
Beaverbooks, Ltd.
150 Lesmill Road
Don Mills, Ontario M3B 2T5
Canada

ACKNOWLEDGMENTS

The thoughtful efforts of a great many people went into the preparation of Contemporary Books' *Building Basic Skills* series. We gratefully acknowledge their contributions and continued involvement in Adult Education.

Adult Education Division

Lillian J. Fleming, Editorial Director
Barbara Drazin, Editor
Wendy Harris, Marketing Services Coordinator

Production Department

Deborah Eisel, Production Editor

Reading and Readability Editors

Jane L. Evanson   Deborah Nathan
Helen B. Ward   Jane Friedland
Norma Libman   Donna Wynbrandt

Authors and Contributors

Writing: Rob Sax

Social Studies: Robert Schambier
Carol Hagel
Phil Smolik
Jack Lesar
Nora Ishibashi
Helen T. Bryant
Jo Ann Kawell
Deborah Brewster
Mary E. Bromage
Sheldon B. Silver
Patricia Miripol

Science: Ronald LeMay
Cynthia Talbert
Jeffrey Miripol
John Gloor
William Collien
Charles Nissim-Sabat

Reading: Timothy A. Foote
Raymond Traynor
Pamela D. Drell (Editor)

Mathematics: Jerry Howett

Project Assistance
Sara Plath

Graphic Art: Louise Hodges
Cover Design: Jeff Barnes

CONTENTS

TO THE LEARNER

HOW TO USE THIS BOOK

Building Basic Skills in Writing, Books 1 and 2 have been planned to give you what you need to master the basics of writing well.

BUILDING BASIC SKILLS IN WRITING	
Book 1	**Book 2**
Sentences	More About Sentences
Nouns	Punctuation
Verbs	Style
More About Verbs	Practical Writing
Pronouns	Spelling
Adjectives and Adverbs	

Together, the books give a complete program that is easy to use on your own or with a teacher in class.

Both books start with a short **Pre-Test.** The questions on the Pre-Test give you an idea of what you'll study in the book. They will also show you the writing skills you already have and those you need to build.

Both books end with a **Post-Test.** By taking the Post-Test after you have worked through the whole book, you will see how much your work has strengthened your skills. Use the **Test-Score Record** on page 9 to keep track of how you do on both Pre-Test and Post-Test.

You will find that *Building Basic Skills in Writing* is an easy, enjoyable way to study. All answers for the Pre-Test and Post-Test are given and explained. Answers to all of the exercises in the book start at the end of each unit. When you finish *Book 1,* you will have no problem moving right on to *Book 2.* Both books will give you all you need to strengthen your basic skills in writing.

WHAT ARE WRITING SKILLS?

Most writing skills are nothing more than common sense. This may surprise you if you have seen English grammar books with hundreds of rules for writing. But all these rules have one simple purpose: They help everyone write English in the same way. Then, what one person writes can be understood by everyone else.

There are differences between speaking and writing. When someone hears you speak, there are many ways to make what you say clear: the look on your face; the way you move your hands; the different ways you say things. From your voice alone, a person can tell if you are serious or if you are joking.

When other people read what you have written, there are none of these clues. The words themselves are all they see. For this reason, written words must be used more carefully than spoken words. Their meanings must be very clear so the reader can understand them. If you keep this idea in mind, many things in this book will be easier to learn.

A good way to learn writing skills is to read a lot. Read everything: school books, comic strips, newspapers, magazines, cereal boxes, advertisements. When you see a new word, write it down in a notebook and find it later in your dictionary. (It is a good idea to buy a dictionary if you don't have one.) Reread your notebook from time to time so you don't forget the new words.

Practice writing whenever you can. Write letters. Start a diary. The more you write, the better.

Writing skills are not hard to master. This book can teach you some of those skills. Your own ideas on writing can be just as important as the ones you will find in this book. Don't be afraid to ask why the rules are as they are. Make writing a part of your life.

The Editors at Contemporary Books

PRE-TEST

Directions: Take the Pre-Test to begin your work in *Building Basic Skills in Writing, Book 2.* The 25 Pre-Test questions test your writing skills in the areas that will be taught in this book. The Pre-Test will also give you an idea of the skills you should strengthen.

Follow the directions for each part. There is no time limit, so you may take as long as you need on each question. When you finish, check your answers. Correct answers start at the end of the Pre-Test. Fill in the Test Score Record for the Pre-Test. It is on page 9. Save this record to see how your skills change after you work through Book 2 and take the the Post-Test.

1 MORE ABOUT SENTENCES

These sentences may be poorly written. One of the numbered choices may be better. If so, put a check mark (✔) next to the choice that is better. If no numbered choice is better, check number (5) no change.

1. He recalled his visit with his brother in the shower.

    _____(1) While in the shower, he recalled a visit with his brother.

    _____(2) He thought about his visiting his brother in the shower.

    _____(3) He thought about his visit, in the shower, to his brother.

    _____(4) He thought about his visit to his brother in the shower.

    _____(5) no change

2. Diane lay down after playing tennis all day on the couch.

_____(1)   Diane, after laying down playing tennis all day on the couch.

_____(2)   Diane lay down, after playing tennis all day on the couch.

_____(3)   Diane lay down on the couch after playing tennis all day.

_____(4)   Diane, after playing tennis all day on the couch, lay down.

_____(5)   no change

3. While walking across the street.

_____(1)   While having walked across the street.

_____(2)   Bill while having walked across the street.

_____(3)   While on his way across the street.

_____(4)   While walking across the street, Bill met Lisa.

_____(5)   no change

4. Kenny married a woman who went to school with my wife.

_____(1)   Kenny married a woman what went to school with my wife.

_____(2)   Kenny married a woman which went to school with my wife.

_____(3)   Kenny married a woman, she went to school with my wife.

_____(4)   Kenny married a woman, the woman went to school with my wife.

_____(5)   no change

5. The lights went out, even though the electricity failed.

_____(1)   Even though the lights went out, the electricity failed.

_____(2)   The lights went out because the electricity failed.

_____(3)   The lights, even though the electricity failed, went out.

_____(4)   The lights went out unless the electricity failed.

_____(5)   no change

2 PUNCTUATION

Four punctuation marks are underlined in each sentence. One may be wrong. If so, write its number in the space given. Do not correct it. If no word is wrong, write 5 in the space.

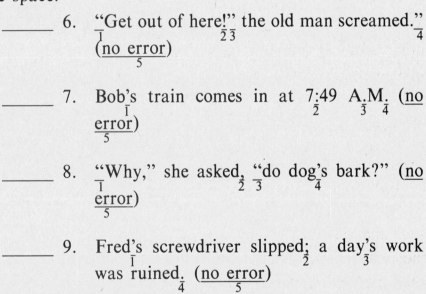

_____ 6.   "Get out of here!" the old man screamed."
           1   2 3   4
           (no error)
              5

_____ 7.   Bob's train comes in at 7:49 A.M. (no
              1   2   3 4
           error)
             5

_____ 8.   "Why," she asked, "do dog's bark?" (no
              1   2   3   4
           error)
             5

_____ 9.   Fred's screwdriver slipped; a day's work
              1   2   3
           was ruined. (no error)
                  4   5

_____10.   U.S. Industries Inc. sells "nuts and bolts"
           1   2   3
           to other manufacturing firms. (no error)
                                     4   5

3 STYLE

These sentences may be poorly written. One of the choices may be better. If so, put a check mark (✔) next to the sentence that is better. If no choice is better, check number 5.

11.   The child follows its mother like a friend.

_____(1)   The child follows its mother like two children.

_____(2)   The child follows its mother like Friday follows Sunday.

_____(3)   The child follows its mother like a surprise.

_____(4)   The child follows its mother like her own shadow.

_____(5)   no change

12.   The chocolate became soft and liquid.

_____(1)   The chocolate melted.

_____(2)   The chocolate became liquid and soft.

_____(3)   The chocolate became fluid and viscous.

_____(4)   The chocolate became soft, and liquid.

_____(5)   no change

13.   He put the book back in the same place where it was when he first happened to find it.

_____(1)   Where it was when he first found it, he put the book back.

_____(2)   He replaced the book in the exact location where it had been originally.

_____(3)   He put the book back where he found it.

_____(4)   He put the book back in the same place where it was when he found it.

_____(5)   no change

14.   The sweater shrank.

_____(1)   The sweater contracted in every dimension.

_____(2) The sweater became smaller than its former size.

_____(3) The sweater diminished.

_____(4) The sweater became little.

_____(5) no change

15. He had liked to fish since he was a boy.

_____(1) He had always been the kind of person who liked to fish since his childhood.

_____(2) Fishing had always been one of his pleasures from the time he was a boy.

_____(3) Ever since his childhood fishing had appealed to him greatly.

_____(4) He had found fishing to be extremely pleasurable since the days of his childhood.

_____(5) no change

4 PRACTICAL WRITING

Here is some information about a woman. Read the information and fill out this application for a savings account for her.

The woman's name is Elizabeth Marie Allen. She was born on November 11, 1954. She lives at 33 Wilson Avenue, Margate. Margate is in Atlantic County. Her zip code is 08402. Margate is in the state of New Jersey. Her telephone number is (609) 765-0025. Her Social Security number is 359-50-2257. She has brown hair and brown eyes. She is 5' 3" tall and weighs 120 lbs. (see page 6)

SAVINGS ACCOUNT—INDIVIDUAL | MARGATE CITY Savings and Loan

16. ACCOUNT IN NAME OF:_____
           (LAST   FIRST   MIDDLE INITIAL)

17. STREET ADDRESS_____

    CITY_____ STATE _____ ZIP CODE _____

18. SOC. SEC. NO. _____TELEPHONE NO. (_____)_____
                                  AREA CODE

PLEASE FILL IN THE FOLLOWING INFORMATION FOR PURPOSES OF IDENTIFICATION ONLY.
                            (CHECK ONE)
                            ☐ MALE

19. HAIR COLOR _____ EYE COLOR _____ ☐ FEMALE

20. HEIGHT ____|____ WEIGHT _____ BIRTH DATE_____
       FT.   IN.   MONTH/DAY/YEAR

---

5   SPELLING

One word in each group may be misspelled. If a word is misspelled, put a check mark (✔) next to it. If no word is misspelled, check number 5.

21. ____(1) nice   ____(2) person   ____(3) adress
    ____(4) lock   ____(5) no error

22. ____(1) second   ____(2) pleasant   ____(3) casual
    ____(4) scissors   ____(5) no error

23. ____(1) naturel   ____(2) simple   ____(3) practical
    ____(4) whistle   ____(5) no error

24. ____(1) ceiling   ____(2) recieve   ____(3) freight
    ____(4) either   ____(5) no error

25. ____(1) tighter   ____(2) quicker   ____(3) hotter
    ____(4) neatter   ____(5) no error

ANSWERS AND EXPLANATIONS—PRE-TEST

1 *More About Sentences*

1. (1) The other sentences make it seem that his visit took place in the shower.
2. (3) The other sentences make it seem that Diane played tennis on the couch.
3. (4) This is the only complete sentence.
4. (5) no change
5. (2) The other sentences make no sense.

2 *Punctuation*

6. (4) There should not be a quotation mark here.
7. (5) no error
8. (4) <u>dog's</u> should be <u>dogs</u>.
9. (5) no error
10. (3) Quotation marks are not needed here.

3 *Style*

11. (4) This is the only comparison that really shows how closely the child follows its mother.
12. (1) <u>melted</u> says in one simple word what <u>soft and liquid</u> says in three.
13. (3) The shortest and simplest way is usually best.
14. (5) no change
15. (5) no change

4 *Practical Writing*

SAVINGS ACCOUNT—INDIVIDUAL	**MARGATE CITY** Savings and Loan

16. ACCOUNT IN NAME OF: *Allen, Elizabeth   M.*
       (LAST)   (FIRST)   MIDDLE INITIAL)

17. STREET ADDRESS *33 Wilson Avenue*

    CITY *Margate*   STATE *New Jersey* ZIP CODE *08402*

18. SOC SEC NO. *359-50-2257* TELEPHONE NO. (*609*) *765-0025*
                                                    AREA CODE

PLEASE FILL IN THE FOLLOWING INFORMATION FOR PURPOSES OF IDENTIFICATION ONLY.

(CHECK ONE)

☐ MALE

19. HAIR COLOR *brown*   EYE COLOR *brown* ☑ FEMALE

20. HEIGHT *5 | 3*   WEIGHT *120* BIRTH DATE *11-11-54*
           FT. IN.   MONTH/DAY/YEAR

5 *Spelling*

21.   (3) adress should be address.

22.   (5) no error

23.   (1) naturel should be natural.

24.   (2) recieve should be receive.

25.   (4) neatter should be neater.

TEST SCORE RECORD

Fill in part of the chart after you take the Pre-Test. Write in the date of your Pre-Test at the bottom of the chart. Then work through the book before taking the Post-Test. After taking the Post-Test fill in the rest of the chart.

	SKILL UNITS	STUDY PAGES	TOTAL	PRE-TEST NUMBER RIGHT	POST-TEST NUMBER RIGHT
1	More About Sentences 1-5	11-40	5		
2	Punctuation 6-10	41-71	5		
3	Style 11-15	72-97	5		
4	Practical Writing 16-20	98-115	5		
5	Spelling 21-25	116-138	5		
	Total		25		

(Date)   (Date)

1 MORE ABOUT SENTENCES

PUT WORDS IN THE RIGHT PLACE

People sometimes write sentences that other people can't understand. One reason is that some of the words are in the wrong place. For example:

> She did her laundry after washing her hair at the laundromat.

Did the woman really wash her hair at the laundromat? Of course not. The writer put some of the words in the wrong place by mistake. He or she meant to write:

> She did her laundry at the laundromat after washing her hair.

Here's another example:

> Sherman fell asleep after playing football all day on the couch.

Was Sherman playing football on the couch? Here is the correct sentence:

> Sherman fell asleep on the couch after playing football all day.

These mistakes are funny, but for some reason they are easy to make.

Exercise 1

Some of the words in these sentences are in the wrong place.

Write the sentences over so that they are correct. The first two have been done as examples.

1. The stewardess slipped and fell as the plane landed on her rear end.

    The stewardess slipped and fell on her rear end as the plane landed.

2. She bandaged her finger after cutting it with a Band-Aid.

    She bandaged her finger with a Band-Aid after cutting it.

3. John told me that his wife killed herself because I asked about her.

    _____

    _____

4. Elise found a book that explains how to climb mountains in the library.

    _____

    _____

5. Mitchell wrote a letter to his brother who had gone to France on airmail paper.

    _____

    _____

6. The preacher read the story of the Hebrews' escape from the Bible.

    _____

    _____

7. Mark and Sue gave their daughter a doll that's so real it wets its pants for Christmas.

---

8. He smacked the dog because it chewed up his shoe with a newspaper.

---

9. The woman had a baby who lives next door.

---

10. My cousin told me how to cook spareribs on the phone.

---

11. The car passed me as I walked down the street at about 60 miles per hour.

---

12. Nancy took out her handkerchief as Ann served the steak and blew her nose in it.

---

13. Diane tried different shades of rouge as her husband sat quietly on her cheeks.

---

14.   The widow cried as the coffin was lowered on her son's shoulder.

_____

_____

15.   The guard put out the fire ten minutes after it started with water.

_____

_____

Answers start on page 34.

FIXING SENTENCES WITH <u>WHILE</u> + <u>ING</u>

Sometimes you can't fix a sentence by just moving the words around. For example:

I picked up a shell walking on the beach.

How can you make clear that I, not the shell, was walking? One way is with the word <u>while</u> and an <u>ing</u>-verb:

<u>While</u> <u>walking</u> on the beach, I picked up a shell.

This sentence was easy to fix. The verb <u>walking</u> was already there. Sometimes, however, you must think up an <u>ing</u>-verb on your own. For example:

Selma likes to watch Johnny Carson in bed with her husband.

It is Selma who is in bed with her husband, not Johnny Carson. How can this be fixed? Ask yourself what Selma was doing. (Let's keep this clean.) She was <u>lying</u>. Use the ing-verb <u>lying</u> and the word <u>while</u> to fix the sentence:

<u>While</u> <u>lying</u> in bed with her husband, Selma likes to watch Johnny Carson.

Exercise 2

These sentences don't make good sense. Use <u>while</u> and an ing-verb to write better ones. The first two have been done as examples.

1. We watched the squirrels eat nuts from the car.

   While sitting in the car, we watched the squirrels eat

   nuts.

2. Marian took the garbage out in her best dress.

   While wearing her best dress, Marian took the gar-

   bage out.

3. The officer saw the plane take off at great speed through his binoculars.

   _____

   _____

4. He thought about his visit to his brother in the bathtub.

   _____

   _____

5. Corey saw Tod make a touchdown from his seat on the sidelines.

   _____

   _____

6.   We heard all about the men who robbed the bank over the radio.

_____

_____

7.   I learned that Mabel and Henry are getting divorced today at the beauty parlor.

_____

_____

8.   I met a woman who had been to China at the supermarket.

_____

_____

9.   Stacy learned how Columbus sailed across the Atlantic Ocean in a book.

_____

_____

10.   We found out that Jack's dog got rabies from our neighbor.

_____

_____

11.   She hummed a song about love in the dentist's waiting room.

_____

_____

12.   She found a picture of her husband fishing for trout in her wallet.

_____

_____

13. She could only think of how she first fell in love with him at his funeral.

_____

_____

14. Harry met a man who had traveled around the world at the barber shop.

_____

_____

15. The children learned how women get pregnant in sex education class.

_____

_____

Answers start on page 35.

GLUING SENTENCES TOGETHER WITH <u>AND</u> & <u>BUT</u>

The sentences in this book are very short to make them easy to read. Most books and newspapers use longer sentences. Longer sentences can be more graceful. Longer sentences can say thoughts which are hard to say in short sentences.

An easy way to make longer sentences is by sticking two short sentences together. How can sentences be glued together? When they have the same verb, sentences can be glued with the word <u>and</u>:

John loves his wife.
Mark loves his wife, too.

These sentences have the same verb, <u>loves</u>, so they can be glued together with <u>and</u>:

John and Mark love their wives.

Notice that some of the words had to be changed. Here is another example. This time the verbs are different, but the subject is the same:

> Cynthia hates men.
> Cynthia dislikes women.

These can be combined to make:

> Cynthia hates men and dislikes women.

Sometimes it makes more sense to use <u>but</u> instead of <u>and</u>. For example:

> Cynthia hates adults.
> Cynthia loves children.

The word <u>but</u> seems to make more sense here:

> Cynthia hates adults but loves children.

Exercise 3

Here are some pairs of short sentences. Use <u>and</u> or <u>but</u> to glue them together. Write the new sentences on the lines. The first two have been done as examples.

1. Howie opened the door. Then he looked into the room.

   Howie opened the door and then looked into the room.

2. Wool shrinks in hot water. Nylon does not shrink.

   Wool shrinks in hot water but nylon does not.

3. April asked her boss for a raise. Her friend Bess did too.

   _____

4. Karen yelled at her husband. She got a sore throat.

_____

_____

5. Andy was denied parole. Clyde was granted parole.

_____

_____

6. We walked in the woods. We got poison ivy.

_____

_____

7. Millicent is sick. She is going to work anyway.

_____

_____

8. Elevators make Hugh nervous. Pretty girls also make him nervous.

_____

_____

_____

9. Charlotte wanted to finish high school. She couldn't.

_____

_____

_____

10. She screams a lot. She doesn't really mean it.

_____

_____

11. Nancy works hard all day. She never misses her favorite TV soap opera.

_____

_____

_____

12. Bacon is high in cholesterol. Eggs are also high in cholesterol.

_____

_____

13. We looked everywhere. We didn't find your glasses.

_____

_____

14. Ted is short. So is Sam.

_____

_____

15. Dogs see poorly. Dogs hear better than people.

_____

_____

Answers start on page 36.

MORE GLUE WORDS

The words <u>and</u> and <u>but</u> are called glue words because they can hold two sentences together. There are many other glue words. <u>Because</u> can be a glue word:

The lights went out. The fuse blew.
The lights went out <u>because</u> the fuse blew.

Exercise 4

Here is a list of glue words:

until	so that	after	if
since	before	while	when
even though	because	unless	where

Use these glue words to join the following pairs of sentences. The first two have been done as examples.

1. Harry went to the movie. He had seen it already.

   Harry went to the movie even though he had seen it

   already.

2. I'll wait here. You come back.

   I'll wait here until you come back.

3. She'll marry you. You ask her.

   _____

   _____

4. We can buy the lamp shade. We bought the other one last year.

   _____

   _____

5. Beryl recovered from her cold. She took the new medicine.

   _____

   _____

6. You should call your brother. You have a better idea.

    _____

7. Put the mouse trap on a high shelf. The baby can't reach it.

    _____

8. I've hated fish. I went to that terrible restaurant.

    _____

    _____

9. I saved one for you. You asked me to.

    _____

    _____

10. She had long hair. She was 20 years old.

    _____

    _____

11. She stays home. He goes to Charlie's house to play poker.

    _____

    _____

12. Her father gets angry. She comes home after midnight.

    _____

    _____

13. She often surprises me. We have been married 22 years.

_____

_____

14. We don't go to the beach. My husband is allergic to sand.

_____

_____

15. Mary stopped seeing Mark. She found out he was a drug addict.

_____

_____

Answers start on page 36.

GLUE WORDS AT THE BEGINNING

Glue words like <u>because</u>, <u>until</u>, and <u>unless</u> can go at the beginning of a sentence. For example:

> He'll be here tomorrow <u>unless</u> something happens to him.
> <u>Unless</u> something happens to him, he'll be here tomorrow.

When the glue word moves to the beginning, the second part of the sentence goes with it. Here are two more examples:

> The second part of the sentence goes with it <u>when</u> the glue word moves to the beginning.
> <u>When</u> the glue word moves to the beginning, the second part of the sentence goes with it.

My father had all his hair <u>until</u> he was fifty-three.

<u>Until</u> he was fifty-three, my father had all his hair.

When the glue word is at the beginning, you need a comma (,) between the two halves of the sentence.

Exercise 5

Here are some sentences with glue words in the middle. Rewrite the sentences so the glue words are at the beginning. Don't forget to add the commas. The first two have been done as examples.

1. We brought you red wine since we know you like it.

    Since we know you like it, we brought you red wine.

2. You cannot eat dessert until you finish your spinach.

    Until you finish your spinach, you cannot eat dessert.

3. I'll find you wherever you are.

    _____

    _____

4. She was ill for three days because she didn't want to go to school.

    _____

    _____

5. He won't shave off his beard even though his wife likes him better without it.

    _____

    _____

6.   Some people feel sleepy after they eat dinner.

_____

_____

7.   We can have a picnic if it doesn't rain.

_____

_____

8.   This program is interrupted due to circumstances beyond our control.

_____

_____

_____

9.   He is nasty regardless of how you speak to him.

_____

_____

10. Burglars broke into the house while the dog was asleep.

_____

_____

Answers start on page 37.

HALF-SENTENCES

People sometimes write sentences which start with glue words and look like these:

After putting the book down.
Because I love you.
No matter what he does.

These sentences are really only half-sentences or sentence fragments. When a sentence starts with a glue word, it needs a comma and a second half. These three half-sentences could be finished like this:

> After putting the book down, he yawned.
> Because I love you, I put up with you.
> No matter what he does, it isn't good
>   enough for her.

Exercise 6

Here are some half-sentences that start with glue words. Finish each one with a comma and a second half. The first two have been done as examples.

1. Even though he's broke

   Even though he's broke, he spends money like a

   millionaire.

2. Whenever you're back in town

   Whenever you're back in town, give me a call.

3. Until he leaves for Seattle

   _____

   _____

4. If my grandmother were a man

   _____

   _____

5. Where I come from

   _____

   _____

6. Although she is supposed to start work at eight

_____

_____

7. Because he got a new job

_____

_____

8. Unless you have a better idea

_____

_____

9. In order to commit the perfect crime

_____

_____

10. When children are young

_____

_____

11. When I get back from lunch

_____

_____

12. Before you told me that

_____

_____

13. Even though Peggy is a woman

_____

_____

14. Because there is no union where he works

_____

_____

15. Since green is her favorite color

_____

_____

Answers start on page 38.

WHICH AND WHO

You can always add information to a sentence with which and who. For example, take this sentence:

Charlie finished his coffee and thanked his host.

Suppose you want to add that the coffee was lousy? Put the word which after the word coffee and add the information. Then go on with the sentence.

Charlie finished his coffee, which was lousy, and thanked his host.

Notice that you have to put commas around the new part of the sentence.

You can also add information about the host. Since the host is a person, you have to use the word who.

Charlie finished his coffee, which was lousy, and thanked his host, who walked him to the door.

If you wanted, you could go on further.

> Charlie finished his coffee, which was lousy, and thanked his host, who walked him to the door, <u>which was already open</u>.

Remember: <u>Who</u> is used to add information about people; <u>which</u> is used for things.

Exercise 7

One word is underlined in each sentence. Add information about that word with <u>who</u> or <u>which</u>. Remember to use commas. The first two have been done as examples.

1. We got married in <u>New Orleans</u>.

   We got married in New Orleans, which is where Jill's

   parents live.

2. I know <u>Judy</u> better than I know her sister.

   I know Judy, who is married to my boss, better than

   I know her sister.

3. This <u>raise</u> will be the first since 1951.

   _____

   _____

4. I got this ring from my <u>grandmother</u>.

   _____

   _____

5.   When will you be back from <u>Chicago</u>?

_____

_____

6.   She's as stupid as <u>Mary</u>.

_____

_____

7.   I like that lamp better than this <u>one</u>.

_____

_____

8.   She says her hobby is <u>photography</u>.

_____

_____

9.   When my <u>father</u> was a young man, he worked as a freak in a circus sideshow.

_____

_____

10.   I lost the <u>bet</u>.

_____

_____

11.   Have you seen <u>Ellen</u>, or has she left?

_____

_____

12. I like your <u>dog</u> more than I like cockroaches.

_____

_____

13. <u>Richard Nixon</u> was the only American president who resigned.

_____

_____

14. Tell me more about your new <u>car</u>.

_____

_____

15. You should put in a new <u>oil filter</u> with every other oil change.

_____

_____

Answers start on page 39.

REVIEW EXERCISE—MORE ABOUT SENTENCES

These sentences are unclear, or incomplete, or poorly written in some other way. Rewrite them so they are clear and complete. Feel free to add to them where needed.

1. We talked to a man who had gone to France by telephone.

_____

_____

2.   After twenty years of marriage.

_____

_____

3.   Tracy has a friend which goes to school with us.

_____

_____

4.   We saw a deer driving along the road.

_____

_____

5.   Unless you have a better idea.

_____

_____

6.   Oliver read that Balboa discovered the Pacific Ocean in his history book.

_____

_____

7.   Toby likes to play poker, so does her husband.

_____

_____

8.   Where the baby can't reach.

_____

_____

9. She carries a photo of her baby playing with finger paints in her wallet.

_____

_____

10. There are 200 old oak trees in this park who was planted in 1784.

_____

_____

ANSWERS AND EXPLANATIONS—MORE ABOUT SENTENCES

Exercise 1

1. The stewardess slipped and fell on her rear end as the plane landed.

2. She bandaged her finger with a Band-Aid after cutting it.

3. Because I asked about his wife, John told me that she killed herself.

4. Elise found a book in the library that explains how to climb mountains.

5. Mitchell wrote a letter on airmail paper to his brother who had gone to France.

6. The preacher read the story from the Bible of the Hebrews' escape.

7. Mark and Sue gave their daughter a doll for Christmas that's so real it wets its pants.

8. He smacked the dog with a newspaper because it chewed up his shoe.

9. The woman who lives next door had a baby.

10. My cousin told me on the phone how to cook spareribs.

11. The car passed me at about 60 miles an hour as I walked down the street.

12. Nancy took out her handkerchief and blew her nose in it as Ann served the steak.

13. Diane tried different shades of rouge on her cheeks as her husband sat quietly.

14. The widow cried on her son's shoulder as the coffin was lowered.

15. The guard put out the fire with water ten minutes after it started.

Exercise 2

1. While sitting in the car, we watched the squirrels eat nuts.

2. While wearing her best dress, Marian took the garbage out.

3. While looking through his binoculars, the officer saw the plane take off at great speed.

4. While sitting in the bathtub, he thought about his visit to his brother.

5. While watching from his seat on the sidelines, Corey saw Tod make a touchdown.

6. While listening to the radio, we heard all about the men who robbed the bank.

7. While having my hair done at the beauty parlor today, I learned that Mabel and Henry are getting divorced.

8. While shopping at the supermarket, I met a woman who had been to China.

9. While reading a book, Stacy learned how Columbus sailed across the Atlantic Ocean.

10. While talking with our neighbor, we found out that Jack's dog got rabies.

11. While sitting in the dentist's waiting room, she hummed a song about love.

12. While looking through her wallet, she found a picture of her husband fishing for trout.

13. While attending his funeral, she could only think of how she first fell in love with him.

14. While getting his hair cut at the barber shop, Harry met a man who had traveled around the world.

15. While studying in sex education class, the children learned how women get pregnant.

Exercise 3

Your sentences may be slightly different.

1. Howie opened the door and then looked into the room.
2. Wool shrinks in hot water but nylon does not.
3. April and Bess asked their bosses for raises.
4. Karen yelled at her husband and got a sore throat.
5. Andy was denied parole, but Clyde was granted it.
6. We walked in the woods and got poison ivy.
7. Millicent is sick but is going to work anyway.
8. Elevators and pretty girls make Hugh nervous.
9. Charlotte wanted to finish high school but couldn't.
10. She screams a lot but doesn't really mean it.
11. Nancy works hard all day but never misses her favorite TV soap opera.
12. Bacon and eggs are high in cholesterol.
13. We looked everywhere but didn't find your glasses.
14. Ted and Sam are short.
15. Dogs see poorly but hear better than people.

Exercise 4

You might have written your answers differently. Check them with a friend.

1. Harry went to the movie even though he had seen it already.
2. I'll wait here until you come back.
3. She'll marry you if you ask her.
4. We can buy the lamp shade where we bought the other one last year.
5. Beryl recovered from her cold because she took the new medicine.
6. You should call your brother unless you have a better idea.

7. Put the mouse trap on a high shelf <u>where</u> the baby can't reach it.

8. I've hated fish <u>since</u> I went to that terrible restaurant.

9. I saved one for you <u>because</u> you asked me to.

10. She had long hair <u>when</u> she was 20 years old.

11. She stays home <u>while</u> he goes to Charlie's house to play poker.

12. Her father gets angry <u>if</u> she comes home after midnight.

13. She often surprises me <u>even though</u> we have been married 22 years.

14. We don't go to the beach <u>because</u> my husband is allergic to sand.

15. Mary stopped seeing Mark <u>after</u> she found out he was a drug addict.

Exercise 5

1. Since we know you like it, we brought you red wine.

2. Until you finish your spinach, you cannot eat dessert.

3. Wherever you are, I'll find you.

4. Because she didn't want to go to school, she was ill for three days.

5. Even though his wife likes him better without it, he won't shave off his beard.

6. After they eat dinner, some people feel sleepy.

7. If it doesn't rain, we can have a picnic.

8. Due to circumstances beyond our control, this program is interrupted.

9. Regardless of how you speak to him, he is nasty.

10. While the dog was asleep, burglars broke into the house.

Exercise 6

There are many ways to answer this exercise. Here is one way.

1. Even though he's broke, he spends money like a millionaire.

2. Whenever you're back in town, give me a call.

3. Until he leaves for Seattle, we will see each other every day.

4. If my grandmother were a man, I would not be talking to you now.

5. Where I come from, things were done differently.

6. Although she is supposed to start work at eight, we rarely see her until ten.

7. Because he got a new job, he bought some new furniture.

8. Unless you have a better idea, let's go to a movie.

9. In order to commit the perfect crime, you have to do it without anyone knowing.

10. When children are young, they need lots of extra attention.

11. When I get back from lunch, I'm too sleepy to work.

12. Before you told me that, I liked you better.

13. Even though Peggy is a woman, she still laughs at things a child finds funny.

14. Because there is no union where he works, they will not go on strike.

15. Since green is her favorite color, she keeps a lot of money around.

Exercise 7

There are many ways to do this exercise correctly. Here is one way.

1. We got married in <u>New Orleans</u>, which is where Jill's parents live.

2. I know <u>Judy</u>, who is married to my boss, better than I know her sister.

3. This <u>raise</u>, which starts on Friday, will be the first since 1951.

4. I got this ring from my <u>grandmother</u>, who had very big fingers.

5. When will you be back from <u>Chicago</u>, which is where Leah lives?

6. She's as stupid as <u>Mary</u>, who doesn't even know how to tie her shoes.

7. I like that lamp better than this <u>one</u>, which is too large for the table.

8. She says her hobby is <u>photography</u>, which is easy to learn.

9. When my <u>father</u>, who was only three feet tall, was a young man, he worked as a freak in a circus sideshow.

10. I lost the <u>bet</u>, which was supposed to be a sure thing.

11. Have you seen <u>Ellen</u>, who has my hat, or has she left?

12. I like your <u>dog</u>, which is well trained, more than I like cockroaches.

13. <u>Richard Nixon</u>, who proposed to his wife on their first date, was the only American president who resigned.

14. Tell me more about your new <u>car</u>, which I heard is very sporty.

15. You should put in a new <u>oil filter</u>, which does not cost a lot, with every other oil change.

ANSWERS AND EXPLANATIONS—REVIEW EXERCISE

Some of your answers may be different.

1. We talked by telephone to a man who had gone to France.
2. After twenty years of marriage, he has never done the dishes.
3. Tracy has a friend who goes to school with us.
4. While driving along the road, we saw a deer.
5. Unless you have a better idea, let's both pay for lunch.
6. Oliver read in his history book that Balboa discovered the Pacific Ocean.
7. Toby and her husband like to play poker.
8. Put it where the baby can't reach.
9. She carries a photo in her wallet of her baby playing with finger paints.
10. There are 200 old oak trees, which were planted in 1784, in this park.

2 PUNCTUATION

PERIODS

One way periods are used is to end some sentences. The first letter of the first word in a sentence is always a capital letter.

Exercise 1

Each group of words is made of one, two, or three sentences. Rewrite the groups of words to show the separate sentences. Study the first two.

1. you can save money by buying in quantity things are cheaper when you buy in large amounts

   You can save money by buying in quantity. Things are

   cheaper when you buy in large amounts.

2. people who believe television commercials are being fooled

   People who believe television commercials are being

   fooled.

3. here is one example commercials say that toothpaste stops cavities the truth is that you need dental floss to get your teeth really clean

   _____

   _____

   _____

4. you don't have to be so careful with the baby babies are
    tough

    _____

    _____

5. advertised products are more expensive because the
    companies that make them have to pay for the
    commercials

    _____

    _____

    _____

6. supermarkets often have their own brands the
    supermarket brands are made by the same companies
    that make the expensive brands advertised on television

    _____

    _____

    _____

7. the main difference between the advertised brands and
    the supermarket brands is the price

    _____

    _____

Check your answers before going on.

8. commercials often show actors in white coats this is
    supposed to make what they are saying seem scientific
    it takes more than a white coat to make a scientist

    _____

    _____

    _____

9. a good example is aspirin real scientists say that plain
    aspirin works just as well as all the fancy ones you see
    in commercials

_____

_____

_____

10. people are influenced by commercials even when they
    don't believe them people tend to reach for products
    they see most often in advertisements

_____

_____

_____

11. you can save a lot of money by buying products which
    are not advertised

_____

_____

12. some people think commercials should be against the
    law

_____

_____

Check your answers before going on.

13. another problem with commercials is that they make
    people buy things they don't really want

_____

_____

14. this problem is worst with children they don't have the sense yet to know that the toys they see on television may be junk

_____

_____

_____

15. sociologists worry about the effects of advertising they say that advertising is the way society talks to itself it is never good to lie to yourself

_____

_____

_____

16. people lose faith in magazines and television they know they are reading and seeing lies

_____

_____

17. advertising costs millions of dollars each year we pay for it when we buy the products.

_____

_____

Answers start on page 63.

QUESTION MARKS

A **question mark** (?) is used when something is asked. Use a period when talking about asking.

Asking: What time is it?
Talking about asking: He asked what time it was.

> Asking: What causes cancer?
> Talking <u>about</u> asking: Scientists want to know what causes cancer.

Exercise 2

Put a period or question mark after each sentence.

1. Don't you want to go
2. Where is a good place to buy tires
3. I wonder if God really exists
4. When will they get here
5. She asked if he could help
6. I want to know whether there's enough time
7. Who knows if it's the best way or not
8. Can you do it
9. How much is ten plus nine
10. They know if he took the painting

Check your answers before going on.

11. Would you like a beer
12. He asked if she felt well
13. She wondered what time it was
14. I asked her where she grew up
15. Mark wanted to know if we were married
16. Would you like to dance
17. How old was your father when he died
18. Was your first child a boy or a girl
19. We'd like to know when you will be leaving
20. The experiment will show whether eating salt affects blood pressure

Check your answers before going on.

21.   Do you like rock and roll

22.   How many ounces are in a quart

23.   He asked if we knew Gertrude well

24.   I think you should ask if they like catfish

25.   At what time does the movie start

26.   How do clams mate

27.   I wish I could tell you why the weather is so bad

28.   He wanted to know if you were married

29.   Can't you go a little faster

30.   Who is she

Answers start on page 64.

ABBREVIATIONS

Periods are usually used after abbreviations. An **abbreviation** is a way to write a short form of a word.

Word	Abbreviation
Mister	Mr.
Company	Co.
United States	U.S.
Incorporated	Inc.

Abbreviations need periods even when they are in the middle of a sentence:

Mr. Jones was born in the U.S. and died in Haiti.

If an abbreviation is the last word in a sentence, put only one period after it:

Mr. Jones was born in the U.S.

The period after an abbreviation can be followed by any punctuation mark except another period:

> Did he work for Smuggs & Co.?
> We know Mr. Jones, Jr., Mr. Jones, Sr., and their wives.

Exercise 3

Write in the periods after the abbreviations in these sentences.

1. Mrs Graham arrived on Oct 3.
2. The city was captured in 270 B C
3. The speed limit is 55 m p h
4. They moved from N Y to California.
5. Dear Mr Burkewitz:
6. Franklin D Roosevelt was elected president four times.
7. Pres Gerald Ford was never elected at all.
8. She was born on Apr 20, 1956.
9. He lives at 1928 Smith St in Merrick.
10. Checks should be made out to the Dept of Motor Vehicles.

Check your answers before going on.

11. The story was on pg 4 of vol III.
12. The baby weighs 9 lbs 4 oz
13. He works for J P Johns and Co
14. U S S R stands for Union of Soviet Socialist Republics.
15. Tax returns must be mailed no later than Apr 15.
16. Address your letters to: P O Box 199, Mt Vernon, N Y
17. The church is named for St Ambrose.
18. Gen Dwight Eisenhower was in command of the army.
19. Turn left at the R R crossing.
20. The U N has over 150 member nations.

Answers start on page 65.

QUOTATION MARKS

Quotation marks are used to show someone else's exact words. One pair of marks goes just before the other person's words; a second pair goes just after them.

> Richard Nixon said, "I am not a crook," but he was.

You only need quotation marks if you write the other person's <u>exact</u> words.

> Richard Nixon said he wasn't a crook, but he was.

It's important to put quotation marks in the right place. They can make a big difference in the meaning of a sentence.

> Cathy said, "John is a fool."
> "Cathy," said John, "is a fool."

Notice how commas are used to separate the exact words from the rest of the sentence.

Exercise 4

Write these sentences again on the lines. Put in quotation marks where needed. Not every sentence needs quotation marks. Notice how commas are used.

1. The foreman told him, Get back to work.
    The foreman told him, "Get back to work."

2. The worker told him to mind his own business.
    The worker told him to mind his own business.

3. The foreman asked, Are you tired of working here?

4. The worker replied, What's it to you?

_____

5. The foreman answered that the worker might not be working there much longer if he didn't get back to work.

_____

_____

6. The worker said, If you don't get off my back I'm calling the shop steward.

_____

_____

7. The foreman said, Ten more seconds and you're fired.

_____

Check your answers before going on.

8. Do you love me? she asked.

_____

9. You know I love you, he answered.

_____

10. She asked him to prove he loved her.

_____

11. I always tell you I love you, he complained, and then you never believe me.

_____

_____

12. I can't help it, she explained. I'm insecure.

_____

Check your answers before going on.

13.   His daughter asked him to buy her an ice cream cone.

_____

14.   What kind would you like? he asked. Chocolate or vanilla?

_____

_____

15.   I want both, she said. Chocolate and vanilla.

_____

16.   Are you sure you can eat that much ice cream? he asked.

_____

_____

17.   She said that she could.

_____

Answers start on page 66.

Exercise 5

The following sentences give a rough idea of what someone said. Use your imagination to figure out what the exact words were. Write new sentences with the exact words in quotation marks. Notice how commas are used in the examples.

1.   He told his boss where he could go.

   He told his boss, "You can go to hell."

2.   He told his wife he was sorry.

   "I feel so terrible about it I want to kill myself,"

   he told his wife.

3.   She asked her boss for a raise.

_____

4.   The policeman asked for Mr. Gebber's driver's license.

_____

5.   Mr. Gebber refused to hand it over.

_____

6.   She asked someone how to get to Delancey Street.

_____

7.   The operator gave her the right phone number.

_____

8.   They thanked her parents for the gift.

_____

9.   Your neighbor complained about the noise.

_____

10.   The clerk insulted him at the unemployment office.

_____

11.   She spoke to the cat as if it were a person.

_____

12.   Nancy complimented her on her new dress.

_____

Answers start on page 67.

COMMAS

One use of commas is to divide a series of three or more. Each item in the series except the last has a comma after it.

> She is smart, honest, and sincere.
> He stepped to the left, then to the right, then forward, and then back.

Writers often leave out the comma before the word <u>and</u>. If you follow the rule given here, however, you will always be right.

Exercise 6

Put commas in the correct places. Some sentences don't need any commas.

1. The French flag the American flag and the Tobrian flag are all red white and blue.
2. Nouns verbs adjectives adverbs and prepositions are all parts of speech.
3. What walks on four legs in the morning on two in the afternoon and on three in the evening?
4. I'm cold and hungry.
5. He'd lie steal or cheat if he could get his way.

Check your answers before going on.

6. The judge found him guilty sentenced him to three years and told the guard to take him back to prison.
7. He was allergic to cheese yogurt butter and other milk products.
8. Running swimming and bicycle riding are good forms of exercise.
9. Spring and summer are the wettest seasons in this climate.
10. We looked for it in the drawers under the bed and behind the dresser.

Check your answers before going on.

11. Nothing is certain but death and taxes.
12. After sanding, wood should be painted stained or varnished.

13.   They enjoy sailing tennis bowling hiking and ping pong.
14.   This offer is of interest to all men women and children.
15.   Would you like coffee tea or milk?

Answers start on page 67.

PARENTHESES

Parentheses are used to sneak in words that aren't really needed.

Pam felt much better (she had been sick for
a week) on Monday.
John (the guy I told you about) asked me to
marry him.
My father (God rest his soul) has been dead
12 years.

In every case, the words in parentheses can be left out without hurting the sentence.

Pam felt much better on Monday.
John asked me to marry him.
My father has been dead 12 years.

Parentheses are also used to show that some information is just background information.

Selma cooked us a delicious dinner on
Wednesday. (She used to be a professional
chef.)

Exercise 7

Fill in parentheses wherever they are needed.

1.   I was bitten don't laugh at this by a caterpillar.
2.   John's mother his father is dead lives in Miami.

3. In the winter of '72 that was a cold one we moved to Detroit.

4. My daughter this was my wife's idea is named Hortense.

5. I understand Italian my parents are Italian but can't speak it.

Answers start on page 68.

USING COMMAS TO ADD INFORMATION

You can use commas to add information about a noun. For example:

Lillian was a soprano in her high school choir.

Lillian, my sister's best friend, was a soprano in her high school choir.

Here are some more examples:

Mercury, the closest planet to the sun, is also the smallest.

Susan F. Rogers, first woman to win the Nobel Prize in Medicine, died last week at age 78.

We talked about our favorite topic, money.

Exercise 8

Use commas to add information about the underlined nouns. Write your new sentences on the lines.

1. The television set is broken.

   The television set, my husband's best friend, is broken.

2. Rodney likes to leave big tips.

    Rodney, a cab driver, likes to leave big tips.

---

3. The world series is over.

---

4. Vermont is beautiful this time of year.

---

5. Janice has been married five times.

---

6. My wife's hobby takes up a lot of her time.

---

7. Marjorie used to work in Bridgeport.

---

8. Doug's car is in the shop again.

---

9. The ship was four days late.

---

10. My dentist charges a lot, but he's good.

---

11. Jessica has a lovely smile.

---

12. Mae West was famous in the thirties.

Answers start on page 68.

THE SEMICOLON

The semicolon smooths things out. Take this example:

He came. He saw. He conquered.

It sounds choppy, doesn't it? There are too many short sentences. The **semicolon** hooks short sentences together into one long one:

He came; he saw; he conquered.

You can only put semicolons between groups of words that can be sentences by themselves. Otherwise, use commas.

WRONG: Whenever you like; I will be there.
RIGHT: Whenever you like, I will be there.

Exercise 9

Join the groups of words with semicolons or commas. If both groups of words are sentences, use a semicolon; otherwise, use a comma. Remember that a sentence must have a subject and a verb; it must also assert something.

1. Seymour lost his temper   he punched his boss in the nose.

    Seymour lost his temper; he punched his boss in the

    nose.

2. At the appropriate time   something can be arranged.

    At the appropriate time, something can be arranged.

3. Julian took notice   all his ideas changed.

_____

4. While looking for a pencil   Nathan found the letter.

_____

5. Andy thought Ellen was perfect   he was in love.

_____

6. Leslie likes Scotch   she won't refuse gin.

_____

7. Amanda was afraid to pick up her baby   she thought it was fragile.

_____

_____

8. When I heard the news   I changed my mind.

_____

Check your answers before going on.

9. I met him once before   once was enough.

_____

10. The letter was returned   the address was wrong.

_____

11. Although I love her   I can't live with her.

_____

12. Speak of what you know   hide what you know not.

_____

Check your answers before going on.

13.   Without makeup   she's even prettier.

_____

14.   We met in Venice   we married in Rome.

_____

15.   The next time I'm up for parole   I'm going to be cool.

_____

16.   Getting unemployment checks is awful   they treat you like garbage.

_____

_____

17.   Malcolm reached   he missed.

_____

Answers start on page 69.

MORE ABOUT COMMAS

Sometimes sentences become so long they get hard to read. For example:

> He knew everything about her including the fact that she had been in prison from talking to her sister but he loved her anyway and still wanted to marry her.

It's hard to read, isn't it? A few commas make it easier:

> He knew everything about her, including the fact that she had been in prison, from talking to her sister, but he loved her anyway and still wanted to marry her.

The commas show which words go together, and make the sentence easier to read and understand.

Exercise 10

Put commas in the following sentences.

1. It took me a while to make up my mind but now I have made it up and the answer is no whether you like it or not.
2. They agreed that she would meet him in Aborville unless it rained in which case he would go to Snydertown because he had a car and she did not.
3. Winning is important in many things including football and love but it's not everything according to many people.
4. I have often thought as I get older that I could have been happier when I was younger if I had known when I was younger what I know now that I am older.
5. When a sentence gets too long it gets hard to understand and although you can fix it with commas it's usually better to make the long sentence into several shorter ones so that the reader won't get lost.
6. Hundreds of years ago very long sentences were popular and if you look in old books such as books written at the time of the American Revolution you will see sentences that cover a whole page and even two or three pages.
7. I told her I wanted to lend them the money not give it to them outright and if she can't understand that there's either something wrong with her hearing or else she just doesn't want to understand what I'm saying.
8. We hold these truths to be self evident: that all men are created equal that they are endowed by their creator with certain unalienable rights and that among these

rights are life liberty and the pursuit of happiness.

9. If you find punctuation hard to learn don't give up because if you keep working at it you'll learn it sooner or later.

10. If you want to fight about it she told him then I'll be glad to keep fighting about it but if you want to forget it and make up I think that would be better.

Answers start on page 70.

TIMES AND DATES

Here are examples of the correct ways to write times and dates:

8:10 a.m.	October 20, 1980
7:45 p.m.	Nov. 6, 1971
12:00 noon	Jan. 7, 1872

Exercise 11

Practice writing times and dates by answering the following questions.

1. What time is it now?   _____
2. What is today's date?   _____
3. What day were you born?   _____
4. What time did you get up today?   _____
5. What time do you usually eat lunch?   _____
6. What's the first day of this year?   _____
7. What day is April Fool's Day this year?   _____
8. What time do you usually go to bed?   _____
9. Give one date that's a holiday this year.   _____
10. What time did you wake up last Sunday?   _____

Answers start on page 71.

REVIEW EXERCISE—PUNCTUATION

These sentences contain errors in punctuation. Rewrite them so they are correct.

1.   She asked us, if we knew the time?

_____

2.   Mrs Lewis "said, I thought the movie was terrific."

_____

3.   Alaska the largest state is the least densely populated.

_____

_____

4.   The movie started at 7;20 pm., we arrived at 7;30.

_____

5.   His opinion changed completely; in light of the new facts.

_____

_____

6.   We were married on Apr 8 1971 had our first child two years later and got divorced in 1975.

_____

_____

7.   Whiskey beer and cigarettes do not make a balanced meal,

_____

_____

8. George my sister's boyfriend told us "to mind our own business."

_____

_____

9. In the summer of 1976 that was a hot one we decided to move north.

_____

_____

10. The baby weighed, 7 lbs at birth.

_____

ANSWERS AND EXPLANATIONS—PUNCTUATION

Exercise 1

1. You can save money by buying in quantity. Things are cheaper when you buy in large amounts.
2. People who believe television commercials are being fooled.
3. Here is one example. Commercials say that toothpaste stops cavities. The truth is that you need dental floss to get your teeth really clean.
4. You don't have to be so careful with the baby. Babies are tough.
5. Advertised products are more expensive because the companies that make them have to pay for the commercials.
6. Supermarkets often have their own brands. The supermarket brands are made by the same companies that make the expensive brands advertised on television.
7. The main difference between the advertised brands and the supermarket brands is the price.
8. Commercials often show actors in white coats. This is supposed to make what they are saying seem scientific. It takes more than a white coat to make a scientist.
9. A good example is aspirin. Real scientists say that plain aspirin works just as well as all the fancy ones you see in commercials.
10. People are influenced by commercials even when they don't believe them. People tend to reach for products they see most often in advertisements.
11. You can save a lot of money by buying products which are not advertised.
12. Some people think commercials should be against the law.

13. Another problem with commercials is that they make people buy things they don't really want.
14. This problem is worst with children. They don't have the sense yet to know that the toys they see on television may be junk.
15. Sociologists worry about the effects of advertising. They say that advertising is the way society talks to itself. It is never good to lie to yourself.
16. People lose faith in magazines and television. They know they are reading and seeing lies.
17. Advertising costs millions of dollars each year. We pay for it when we buy the products.

Exercise 2

1. Don't you want to go?
2. Where is a good place to buy tires?
3. I wonder if God really exists.
4. When will they get here?
5. She asked if he could help.
6. I want to know whether there's enough time.
7. Who knows if it's the best way or not.
8. Can you do it?
9. How much is ten plus nine?
10. They know if he took the painting.

11. Would you like a beer?
12. He asked if she felt well.
13. She wondered what time it was.
14. I asked her where she grew up.
15. Mark wanted to know if we were married.
16. Would you like to dance?
17. How old was your father when he died?
18. Was your first child a boy or a girl?
19. We'd like to know when you will be leaving.

20. The experiment will show whether eating salt affects blood pressure.

21. Do you like rock and roll?
22. How many ounces are in a quart?
23. He asked if we knew Gertrude well.
24. I think you should ask if they like catfish.
25. At what time does the movie start?
26. How do clams mate?
27. I wish I could tell you why the weather is so bad.
28. He wanted to know if you were married.
29. Can't you go a little faster?
30. Who is she?

Exercise 3

1. Mrs. Graham arrived on Oct. 3.
2. The city was captured in 270 B.C.
3. The speed limit is 55 m.p.h.
4. They moved from N.Y. to California.
5. Dear Mr. Burkewitz:
6. Franklin D. Roosevelt was elected president four times.
7. Pres. Gerald Ford was never elected at all.
8. She was born on Apr. 20, 1956.
9. He lives at 1928 Smith St. in Merrick.
10. Checks should be made out to the Dept. of Motor Vehicles.

11. The story was on pg. 4 of vol. III.
12. The baby weighs 9 lbs. 4 oz.
13. He works for J.P. Johns and Co.
14. U.S.S.R. stands for Union of Soviet Socialist Republics.
15. Tax returns must be mailed no later than Apr. 15.

16. Address your letters to: P.O. Box 199, Mt. Vernon, N.Y.
17. The church is named for St. Ambrose.
18. Gen. Dwight Eisenhower was in command of the army.
19. Turn left at the R.R. crossing.
20. The U.N. has over 150 member nations.

Exercise 4

1. The foreman told him, "Get back to work."
2. The worker told him to mind his own business.
3. The foreman asked, "Are you tired of working here?"
4. The worker replied, "What's it to you?"
5. The foreman answered that the worker might not be working there much longer if he didn't get back to work.
6. The worker said, "If you don't get off my back I'm calling the shop steward."
7. The foreman said, "Ten more seconds and you're fired."

8. "Do you love me?" she asked.
9. "You know I love you," he answered.
10. She asked him to prove he loved her.
11. "I always tell you I love you," he complained, "and then you never believe me."
12. "I can't help it," she explained. "I'm insecure."

13. His daughter asked him to buy her an ice cream cone.
14. "What kind would you like?" he asked. "Chocolate or vanilla?"
15. "I want both," she said. "Chocolate and vanilla."
16. "Are you sure you can eat that much ice cream?" he asked.
17. She said that she could.

Exercise 5

Your answers may be different from the sample answers given here.

1. He told his boss, "You can go to hell."
2. "I feel so terrible about it I want to kill myself," he told his wife.
3. "May I have a raise?" she asked her boss.
4. The policeman asked Mr. Gebber, "Do you have your driver's license, sir?"
5. "I'm not showing you anything," said Mr. Gebber.
6. "Can you tell me how to get to Delancey Street?" she asked.
7. "The number is 255-0025," said the operator.
8. "It's just what we wanted," they said. "Thank you very much."
9. Your neighbor screamed, "If you don't turn that down, I'm calling the police."
10. "You look like a slob," said the clerk at the unemployment office.
11. She asked the cat, "Would you like to go to the movies?"
12. "You look nice in that dress," Nancy said.

Exercise 6

1. The French flag, the American flag, and the Tobrian flag are all red, white, and blue.
2. Nouns, verbs, adjectives, adverbs, and prepositions are all parts of speech.
3. What walks on four legs in the morning, on two in the afternoon, and on three in the evening?
4. I'm cold and hungry.
5. He'd lie, steal, or cheat if he could get his way.

6. The judge found him guilty, sentenced him to three years, and told the guard to take him back to prison.
7. He was allergic to cheese, yogurt, butter, and other milk products.
8. Running, swimming, and bicycle riding are good forms of exercise.
9. Spring and summer are the wettest seasons in this climate.
10. We looked for it in the drawers, under the bed, and behind the dresser.

11. Nothing is certain but death and taxes.
12. After sanding, wood should be painted, stained, or varnished.
13. They enjoy sailing, tennis, bowling, hiking, and ping pong.
14. This offer is of interest to all men, women, and children.
15. Would you like coffee, tea, or milk?

Exercise 7

1. I was bitten (don't laugh at this) by a caterpillar.
2. John's mother (his father is dead) lives in Miami.
3. In the winter of '72 (that was a cold one) we moved to Detroit.
4. My daughter (this was my wife's idea) is named Hortense.
5. I understand Italian (my parents are Italian) but can't speak it.

Exercise 8

Your sentences will probably be different. Study these sample sentences.

1. The television set, my husband's best friend, is broken.

2. Rodney, a cab driver, likes to leave big tips.
3. The world series, the last games of the season, is over.
4. Vermont, where Stan lives, is beautiful this time of year.
5. Janice, the friend I told you about, has been married five times.
6. My wife's hobby, playing the piano, takes up a lot of her time.
7. Marjorie used to work in Bridgeport, the city where she grew up.
8. Doug's car, the one that broke down last week, is in the shop again.
9. The ship, the one we wanted to take, was four days late.
10. My dentist, Dr. Weaver on Main Street, charges a lot, but he's good.
11. Jessica, my neighbor's niece, has a lovely smile.
12. Mae West, star of many movies, was famous in the thirties.

Exercise 9

1. Seymour lost his temper; he punched his boss in the nose.
2. At the appropriate time, something can be arranged.
3. Julian took notice; all his ideas changed.
4. While looking for a pencil, Nathan found the letter.
5. Andy thought Ellen was perfect; he was in love.
6. Leslie likes Scotch; she won't refuse gin.
7. Amanda was afraid to pick up her baby; she thought it was fragile.
8. When I heard the news, I changed my mind.
9. I met him once before; once was enough.
10. The letter was returned; the address was wrong.
11. Although I love her, I can't live with her.
12. Speak of what you know; hide what you know not.

13. Without makeup, she's even prettier.

14. We met in Venice; we married in Rome.
15. The next time I'm up for parole, I'm going to be cool.
16. Getting unemployment checks is awful; they treat you like garbage.
17. Malcolm reached; he missed.

Exercise 10

Your answers may be slightly different.

1. It took me a while to make up my mind, but now I have made it up, and the answer is no, whether you like it or not.
2. They agreed that she would meet him in Aborville unless it rained, in which case he would go to Snydertown, because he had a car and she did not.
3. Winning is important in many things, including football and love, but it's not everything, according to many people.
4. I have often thought, as I get older, that I could have been happier when I was younger, if I had known when I was younger what I know now that I am older.
5. When a sentence gets too long, it gets hard to understand, and although you can fix it with commas, it's usually better to make the long sentence into several shorter ones so that the reader won't get lost.
6. Hundreds of years ago very long sentences were popular, and if you look in old books, such as books written at the time of the American Revolution, you will see sentences that cover a whole page and even two or three pages.
7. I told her I wanted to lend them the money, not give it to them outright, and if she can't understand that, there's either something wrong with her hearing or else she just doesn't want to understand what I'm saying.
8. We hold these truths to be self evident: that all men are created equal, that they are endowed by their

creator with certain unalienable rights, and that among these rights are life, liberty, and the pursuit of happiness.

9. If you find punctuation hard to learn, don't give up because if you keep working at it you'll learn it sooner or later.

10. If you want to fight about it, she told him, then I'll be glad to keep fighting about it, but if you want to forget it and make up, I think that would be better.

Exercise 11

Your answers may be different from the samples given here.

1. 7:15 p.m.
2. December 29, 1980
3. June 3, 1945
4. 6:30 a.m.
5. 12:00 noon
6. January 1, 1981
7. April 1, 1975
8. 12:00 midnight
9. December 25, 1981
10. 10:35 a.m.

ANSWERS AND EXPLANATIONS—REVIEW EXERCISE

1. She asked us if we knew the time.
2. Mrs. Lewis said, "I thought the movie was terrific."
3. Alaska, the largest state, is the least densely populated.
4. The movie started at 7:20 p.m.; we arrived at 7:30.
5. His opinion changed completely in light of the new facts.
6. We were married on Apr. 8, 1971, had our first child two years later, and got divorced in 1975.
7. Whiskey, beer, and cigarettes do not make a balanced meal.
8. George, my sister's boyfriend, told us to mind our own business.
9. In the summer of 1976 (that was a hot one) we decided to move north.
10. The baby weighed 7 lbs. at birth.

3 STYLE

Style is partly a matter of personal taste, but there are three rules that everyone should know about. These are:

1. Good writing is <u>succinct</u>; it wastes no words.

2. Good writing is <u>easy to understand</u>.

3. Good writing is <u>concrete and vivid</u>; it gives a strong, clear picture.

CUT THE FAT

Succinct writing is good writing. It is brief and to the point. The best writing uses the fewest words that say what must be said. It's something like going shopping. If $20 will buy what you want, why spend $30? If 20 words will say what you want, why write 30? The fewer words, the better. Cut the fat out. Your writing will be easier to read. Each word will pack more punch. To prove it, look at these two paragraphs:

The second paragraph says twice as much as the first in fewer words. The second paragraph is better written.

1.   There are a good number of people who don't think that luck really exists, but I think that it does. Luck is the only thing I can think of that can explain how the most amazing day that ever happened to me came to pass. While I was walking to work I found lying on the sidewalk in front of me a five dollar bill. It was just lying on the sidewalk. Later, just before lunchtime, I got a phone call from one of my old boy friends. He said that he didn't know why, but he felt that he was in love with me again. After I got back from lunch in the afternoon I got another phone call. This one was from my husband. . .

2.   Some people don't believe in luck, but I do. Only luck can explain the most remarkable day of my life. While walking to work I found a five dollar bill on the sidewalk. Just before lunch my old boyfriend called and said he was in love with me again. In the afternoon my husband called to say the parole board had decided to release him. On my way home from work I found a ten dollar bill on the sidewalk. That night, I learned I had won a contest. My prize was a trip to Hawaii for three.

Exercise 1

Read each sentence. Count the number of words used. Write the number in the blank. Then rewrite the sentence. Make it as short as possible. Make sure your sentence means the same thing as the one given. Then write the number of words <u>you</u> used. The first two have been done.

1.   If you have ever happened to have visited New York, you know that what they say about New Yorkers being unfriendly is not true at all.   __26_ words

If you have been to New York, you know it's not true

that New Yorkers are unfriendly.   <u>17</u> **words**

2. Swimming is one of my absolute favorite activities, one that appeals to me as much as anything in the whole world.   <u>21</u> **words**

I love to swim.   <u>4</u> **words**

3. When you live in America but at the same time you don't speak English, it feels just exactly the same as when you are locked up in prison.   ____ **words**

_____

_____

_____
                                          ____ **words**

4. As soon as tomorrow comes, my friend Joe and I are going to really sit down and figure out what we ought to do about this problem of ours.   ____ **words**

_____

_____

_____
                                          ____ **words**

5. Getting to the point where you can really write well is not the easiest thing in the world.   ____ **words**

_____

_____

_____
                                          ____ **words**

Examples of how you <u>might</u> answer these questions are given at the end of this unit.

Answers start on page 94.

Exercise 2

Common sayings such as <u>don't cry over spilled milk</u> have become common because they are so well written. Each of the following sentences is a common saying which is longer than it needs to be. Figure out the original sayings. Write them on the lines. Count the number of words used each time and write this in the blanks. The first one has been done.

1. Whoever goes to bed early in the evening will also get out of bed early the next morning.   **18** words
   Early to bed, early to rise.   **6** words

2. After the bottle has been knocked over and all the milk has poured out, there's no point in crying about it. ____words

   _____

   _____

   _____
                                                   ____**words**

3. You should treat other people the same way that you would like them to treat you.   ____ **words**

   _____

   _____
                                                   ____**words**

4. Very often when you try to do something quickly, it turns out to take even longer than when you do it slowly.   ____**words**

   _____

   _____
                                                   ____**words**

5. It's better to make love than it is to go off and fight wars.   ____words

_____

_____

                                           ____words

6. If someone pokes out your eye, you ought to poke out his eye, and if he knocks out your tooth, you ought to knock out his tooth.   ____words

_____

_____

                                           ____words

7. Everything that glitters isn't necessarily made of gold. ____words

_____

_____

                                           ____words

8. It is just about impossible to get an old dog to learn to do something new.   ____words

_____

_____

                                           ____words

Answers start on page 94.

FAT PHRASES

One of the enemies of succinct writing is the fat phrase. The fat phrase is full of wasted words. Fat phrases should always be trimmed to the bone to make your writing firmer, stronger, and more graceful.

Fat Phrase	Better Phrase
The question as to whether	Whether . . . .
I did not know the fact that	I did not know . . . .
He is a man who	He . . . .
This is used for defense purposes	This is used for defense . . .
Owing to the fact that	Because . . . .
Being that she	Since she . . . .
In spite of the fact that . . .	Although . . . .

Exercise 3

The following sentences are full of fat phrases. Cross out the wasted words. Then rewrite the sentences so they are shorter. The first one has been done as an example.

1. They ~~are the kind of people who~~ feed their children nothing but potato chips.
   They feed their children nothing but potato chips.

2. In spite of the fact that tax revenues will be lower next year, Congress will spend more.

   _____

   _____

3. Baking soda can be used for cleaning purposes.

   _____

   _____

4. Owing to the fact that she was a woman who didn't know it was raining, she didn't bring an umbrella.

   _____

   _____

5. Scientists don't know the answer to the question whether life exists on other planets.

_____

_____

6. This is a movie that ends up happily.

_____

_____

Answers start on page 95.

BIG WORDS

People often think that good writing uses long, unusual words instead of the short, simple ones of everyday speech. This is fatuity. (Fatuity is the kind of word you should avoid. It means foolishness.) You are writing to be understood, and short words are easier to understand. For this reason, they are also stronger. Unless a longer word is necessary to give the exact meaning you have in mind, use the short one.

> Poor: They queried us about Michael.
> Better: They asked us about Michael.

> Poor: The illumination was deficient.
> Better: The light was dim.

> Poor: The house was constructed in 1878.
> Better: The house was built in 1878.

Good writing is not fancy. It is simple and direct. Here is what Ralph Waldo Emerson had to say on the subject. He is held to be one of the greatest stylists among American writers.

Everyone has felt how superior in force is the language of the street to that of the academy. The speech of the man in the street is invariably strong. You say, "If he could only express himself"; but he does already, better than anyone can for him. The power of his speech is that it is perfectly understood by all. And observe that all poetry is written in the oldest and simplest English words.

Exercise 4

Find short, simple words to replace the underlined words. Use a dictionary if you need to look up the underlined words. The first one has been done as an example.

1. He wagered ten dollars that no one could beat him.   *bet*

2. We endeavored as hard as we could.   _____

3. We have never possessed a car.   _____

4. After lunch we conversed about love.   _____

5. My conception of honesty is different from yours.   _____

6. She elevated the baby from its carriage.   _____

7. We acquired that as a wedding present.   _____

8. This is the termination of the road.   _____

9. They want a female child.   _____

10. Talk is inexpensive.   _____

Answers start on page 95.

USE NOUNS AND VERBS, NOT ADJECTIVES AND ADVERBS

One way to make your writing stronger is to use more nouns and verbs and fewer adjectives and adverbs. Nouns and verbs are the bones and muscles of the language; adjectives and adverbs are extras. A poor writer might say:

The tired man walked home slowly.

But a better writer would put it this way:

The man trudged home.

The verb trudged means to walk slowly as if tired. It puts into one word the meaning of the adjective tired; the adverb slowly, and the verb walked. Here are some other examples:

Poor: He pushed the door sharply.

Better: He shoved the door.

Poor: There was an awful smell.

Better: There was a stench.

Poor: He rubbed her face softly.

Better: He caressed her face.

In each case, the better example uses a single noun or verb that combines the meaning of two words.

push sharply = shove

awful smell = stench

rub softly   = caress

Instead of using a verb and an adverb, it is better to use a single verb that combines their meanings. In the same way, instead of using a noun and an adjective, it is better to use a single noun.

Exercise 5

Rewrite the following sentences so that the underlined words are replaced by single words. The first one has been done as an example. Share these with a friend if you get stumped.

1. He called loudly from the sixth-floor window.
    He shouted from the sixth-floor window.

2. The shirt got smaller in the hot water.

3. The child broke the vase into tiny pieces.

4. The electric impulses last only for a very short time.

5. He frequently speaks haltingly when he's nervous.

6. Millions of people are dying from lack of food.

7. She looked intently into his eyes.

8. She had blue eyes as an extremely young baby.

9. The river travels slowly and indirectly to the sea.

10. He spoke softly and indistinctly into her ear.

Answers start on page 95.

There is a better way to replace adverbs and adjectives with nouns and verbs. In this second way, you replace a description with a little story. Here is a description as it would be written by a poor writer:

On the table was an <u>extremely</u> <u>heavy</u> load.

A better writer might tell this little story instead:

The table <u>sagged</u> under its load.

The verb <u>sagged</u> does not mean the same thing as the adverb and adjective <u>extremely</u> <u>heavy</u>, but nonetheless it takes their place. Here are other examples:

Poor: She was very, very happy.
Better: She laughed and cried at the same time.

Poor: Her skirt was long and tight and narrow at the hem.
Better: She could hardly walk in that skirt.

Poor: The mud was thick and sticky.
Better: The mud sucked our shoes off.

To replace adjectives and adverbs with stories, try to think of what the thing you are describing might <u>do</u>. For example:

The woman's girdle was very tight.

What does a tight girdle do? It might stop her blood flow, or hurt her, or break when she bends over. A good writer might say:

The girdle split when she bent over.

Exercise 6

Make up little stories to replace the adjectives and adverbs in the following sentences. The first one has been done as an example.

1. He was terribly hot and sweaty.
   Sweat ran down his face and neck.

2. He was terribly cold.

3. She was extremely stingy.

4. Things are extremely expensive today.

5. It was an extremely difficult test.

6. She was terribly frightened.

Examples of how you might answer these questions are given in the Answers and Explanations.

Answers start on page 96.

BE CONCRETE

Strong, vivid writing shows details, facts and pictures. It avoids the vague and general. Good writing always gives underline examples of what the writer has in mind.

Poor: The standard of living has risen significant-
ly over the last few decades.

Better: The average worker makes twice as much
today as in 1940.

Poor: The weather was wretched for quite some
time.

Better: It rained for ten days straight.

Poor: He showed considerable anger as he went
out.

Better: He cursed and slammed the door as he left
the room.

One of the best places to look for vivid, concrete writing is the Bible. On the left is a poorly written paragraph. It is full of vague generalities. On the right is the version you will find in the Bible. It is full of concrete examples. (Of course the Bible's language is old-fashioned, but that doesn't affect the quality of its style.)

People don't gain the good things in life according to their abilities; instead, who succeeds and who fails depends in every case on accidents and luck.

The race is not to the swift, nor the battle to the strong, nor bread to the wise, nor riches to the learned, nor favor to the skillful; but time and chance happen to all.

Exercise 7

The following sentences are poorly written because they are not concrete. By making up examples and using your imagination, replace these poor sentences with concrete ones. The first one has been done as an example.

1. She was amused by his bad manners.

   She laughed when he wiped his nose on his sleeve.

2. His luck changed for the worse.

   _____

   _____

3. He was a spectacularly ugly man.

   _____

   _____

4. The union plans to take strong steps to get a better deal.

   _____

   _____

5. She seemed to be nervous.

   _____

   _____

6. The building is run down and needs work badly.

   _____

   _____

Examples of how you might answer these questions are given in the Answers and Explanations.

Answers start on page 96.

COMPARISONS

Writers often spice up their writing with comparisons. In a **comparison,** you describe one thing by saying it is like another. When you say someone is <u>fat</u> <u>as</u> <u>a</u> <u>sausage</u>, or <u>thin</u> <u>as</u> <u>a</u> <u>coat</u> <u>hanger</u>, you are making comparisons.

Some people have a natural talent for making comparisons. You may be one of them. Here are some comparisons that were written by William Shakespeare, a great English poet. A plain way to write the same thing is printed on the left.

A Plain Way to Say It	Shakespeare's Comparison
1. I see a strange expression on your face.	Your face is a book where men may read strange matters.
2. My skin is sagging and wrinkled.	My skin hangs about me like an old lady's loose gown.
3. You should pretend to be sweet and loving, but underneath you should really be fierce and full of hate.	Look like the innocent flower, but be like the serpent under it.

A good comparison often makes the reader see or hear or feel something; it draws a picture. You must be careful, however, that the picture you draw shows the thing you want to show. The following is a poor comparison because the author forgot to keep this in mind.

She was a terrible singer. Her voice was like
gravel and ice mixed together.

Gravel and ice mixed together make a picture, but what do they tell you about the woman's voice? Nothing. Gravel and ice make no sound. The next comparison is better:

> She was a terrible singer. Her voice was like
> the screams of an old rooster being roasted
> alive.

An old rooster being roasted alive makes a picture, too, but it also gives the reader a good idea of what the woman sounded like.

Exercise 8

Make the following comparisons better by replacing the underlined phrases with new phrases of your own. The first two have been done as examples.

1. She stopped crying and smiled. Her smile was like a bird building its nest in a tree.

    Her smile was like *the sun breaking through the clouds after a storm*.

2. He was a huge man. His hands were like whales.
    His hands were like *baseball gloves*.

3. It was hot in the sun, and he was working hard. Sweat poured from his face like feathers from a bird.
    Sweat poured from his face like

    _____

4. He was tall and skinny, and she was short and fat. When they were together they looked like a peach and an apple.
    They looked like

    _____

5. He was the world's worst driver. Driving with him was as dangerous as eating oranges for breakfast.

    Driving with him was as dangerous as
    _____

    _____

6. She never pays anyone back. Lending her money is like shopping early in the morning.

    Lending her money is like
    _____

    _____

7. Studying for the G.E.D. test is no fun. It's as boring as making love for the first time.

    It's as boring as
    _____

    _____

Examples of how you might answer these questions are given in the Answers and Explanations.

Answers start on page 96.

REVIVING DEAD COMPARISONS

Some comparisons are used so often that they have lost their meaning. They have become dead comparisons. For example:

It was hot as hell.

When someone says it was as hot as hell, do you think of fires burning in hell? Probably not. You have heard the phrase too many times. Dead comparisons like this one should not be used, because they call up no picture in the reader's mind.

How can we make the comparison live again? By changing it to make it fresh:

It was hot as a truck's exhaust pipe.

Exercise 9

Put some new life into the following dead comparisons. The first two have been done as examples.

1. The victim was as dead as a doornail.

    dead as *a tin can*

2. Her heart is as cold as ice.

    cold as *the bottom of the Arctic Ocean*

3. Before his heart attack, he was strong as an ox.

    strong as

4. The old man is tough as nails.

    tough as

5. The kitten was as black as coal.

    black as

6. The dog grabbed the steak as fast as lightning.

    fast as

7. The bee sting burned like fire.

    burned like

Examples of how you might answer these questions are given in the Answers and Explanations.

Answers start on page 97.

JARGON

From time to time, whole cities and even countries are struck by disease. Millions are sick at once. An epidemic has broken out.

Languages, too, suffer epidemics. The English language has one today. It's all around you in every book and magazine and newspaper you see, so be careful not to catch it. The name of the disease is jargon.

Jargon is special language used only by a few people. Most jobs and professions have their own jargon. There is baseball jargon:

The first run was knocked in by Horner on a
line drive single to left field.

Doctors' jargon:

A pyogenic granuloma was excised from the
second toe.

Cooks' jargon:

Sauté in light oil over medium heat.

There is nothing wrong with jargon when it's the only way something can be said. There is no other word for line drive single, or for pyogenic granuloma, or for sauté. But jargon becomes a disease when the author only wants to impress people, or when he doesn't know how to say the same thing in ordinary English, or when he purposely uses it to confuse people.

Here are some more examples of jargon. On the right is a better way to say the same thing, using plain English.

Jargon	Good Plain English
1. I'm building my writing skills.	I'm learning to write.
2. Life expectancy is being enhanced in the developing countries.	People are living longer in poor countries.
3. I'm not sure how secure their bonding really is.	I'm not sure they really are in love.

Exercise 10

The following sentences are written in jargon. Change them into plain English. If you don't understand the jargon, use a dictionary. The first one has been done as an example.

1. Male parenting is on the upswing.

   Fathers are spending more time with their children.

   _____

2. The team's win/loss ratio is on a downturn.

   _____

   _____

3. This product contains artificial preservatives to retard spoilage.

   _____

   _____

4. The police are accelerating their apprehension of perpetrators.

_____

_____

5. Research underscores Cecum cigarettes as a proven taste alternative to high tar smoking.

_____

_____

6. A successful transition from childhood to adulthood demands a rejection of parental definitions of identity.

_____

_____

Examples of how you might answer these questions are given in the Answers and Explanations.

Answers start on page 97.

REVIEW EXERCISE—STYLE

The following story is poorly written. Use everything you learned in this chapter to rewrite it. Use a separate sheet of paper.

On a certain day in the month of November, on a Wednesday evening to be more exact, a man walked up the steps of the local high school. He had come for purposes of attending a night class that was given as part of the adult education program.

He had a feeling of nervousness. The palms of his hands were moist like kettles. His heart pounded like a toothache.

As he entered the office, the fear struck him that they would laugh at him. He had never finished his high school education. He imagined that everyone could see that he did not belong in a school environment.

The secretary looked bored. "Can I help you?" she asked.

Finish the story yourself.

ANSWERS AND EXPLANATIONS —STYLE

Exercise 1

Your sentences may be slightly different.

1. 26 words
   If you have been to New York, you know it's not true that New Yorkers are unfriendly.   17 words
2. 21 words
   I love to swim.   4 words
3. 28 words
   Living in America without speaking English is like being in jail.   11 words
4. 29 words
   Tomorrow my friend Joe and I will sit down and solve this problem.   13 words
5. 18 words
   It's not easy to write well.   6 words

Exercise 2

1. 18 words
   Early to bed, early to rise.   6 words
2. 21 words
   There's no use crying over spilled milk.   7 words
3. 16 words
   Do unto others as you would have them do unto you.   11 words
4. 22 words
   Haste makes waste.   3 words
5. 14 words
   Make love, not war.   4 words

6. 27 words
   An eye for an eye, a tooth for a tooth.   10 words
7. 8 words
   All that glitters is not gold.   6 words
8. 16 words
   You can't teach an old dog new tricks.   8 words

Exercise 3

1. They feed their children nothing but potato chips.
2. Although tax revenues will be lower next year, Congress will spend more.
3. Baking soda can be used for cleaning.
4. Because she didn't know it was raining, she didn't bring an umbrella.
5. Scientists don't know whether life exists on other planets.
6. This movie ends happily.

Exercise 4

1. bet
2. tried
3. owned
4. talked
5. idea
6. lifted
7. got
8. end
9. girl
10. cheap

Exercise 5

1. He shouted from the sixth-floor window.
2. The shirt shrank in the hot water.
3. The child shattered the vase.
4. The electric impulses last only for an instant.

5.   He frequently stammers when he's nervous.
6.   Millions of people are dying from starvation.
7.   She stared into his eyes.
8.   She had blue eyes as an infant.
9.   The river wanders to the sea.
10. He murmured into her ear.

Exercise 6

Your answers may be different from these examples.

1.   Sweat ran down his face and neck.
2.   His teeth chattered.
3.   She gave the Red Cross five cents every year.
4.   John paid $15 for a cucumber today.
5.   Ninety-nine out of 100 people failed the test.
6.   She fainted from fear.

Exercise 7

Your sentences may be very different from these.

1.   She laughed when he wiped his nose on his sleeve.
2.   After he lost everything in the flood, his best friend stole his girl.
3.   Babies cried when they saw him.
4.   The union will walk out at 4 o'clock to win a raise.
5.   She was afraid to look them in the eye and spoke in a whisper.
6.   There is a hole in the porch and the furnace is broken.

Exercise 8

Your sentences may be very different from these.

1.   Her smile was like the sun breaking through the clouds after a storm.
2.   His hands were like baseball gloves.
3.   Sweat poured from his face like rain off a roof.

4. They looked like a toothpick and a pound cake.
5. Driving with him was as dangerous as petting a mad dog.
6. Lending her money is like throwing away cash.
7. It's as boring as watching a test signal on television.

Exercise 9

Your answers may be very different.

1. dead as a tin can
2. cold as the bottom of the Arctic Ocean
3. strong as an Olympic athlete
4. tough as a vault door
5. black as ebony
6. fast as the blink of an eye
7. burned like a hot needle

Exercise 10

Your answers may be different from these examples.

1. Fathers are spending more time with their children.
2. The team has been winning fewer games.
3. There are chemicals in this food to make it last longer.
4. The police are speeding up the arrest of criminals.
5. Studies show that Cecum cigarettes taste just as good as cigarettes that are higher in tar.
6. Successful growing up demands knowing who you are. *or* To grow up, you have to decide for yourself who you are.

ANSWERS AND EXPLANATIONS—REVIEW EXERCISE

Each story will be different. Make sure yours is clear and well written. Read it aloud to another person.

4 PRACTICAL WRITING

FILLING OUT FORMS

If you're like most people, you often have to fill out forms.

A **form** is a piece of paper that asks you for information. A form has instructions printed on it which say how you should show the information. Sometimes it has a space for you to fill in.:

City	State	Zip

City *Chicago,*	State *Il.*	Zip *60615*

Sometimes forms have boxes for you to check:

☐ Mr.
☑ Mrs.
☐ Miss

Where numbers must be shown, forms sometimes give you boxes:

Date of Birth:

| 0 | 9 | 0 | 1 | 4 | 6 |

The date above is September (the ninth month) 1, 1946.

Exercise 1

1. On the following pages are two samples of a direct-mail order blank from a catalog. The first has been filled in so you can see how to do it. The second is for you to fill in. Fill in the spaces for NAME AND ADDRESS and METHOD OF PAYMENT. Then fill in the ordering information. The direct-mail order blank asks you to give the CATALOG NUMBER, HOW MANY you want, COLOR NO. (number) OR SIZE, TOTAL PRICE, and SHPG. WT. (shipping weight) of everything you order. This information comes from the store catalog. We can't print the catalog information here, so make up that information yourself. Fill out the form as if you were ordering something you use around your home. This could be tools, furniture, linens, or other household items.

SEARS, ROEBUCK AND CO. *Satisfaction Guaranteed or Your Money Back*

	DAY	ORDERS	# LINES	SOURCE OF SALE	TYPE SALE	METHOD SHIPMT	CASH	DISCT.	TAX EXMT.	SPEC CODE	SPECIAL INFORMATION (DO NOT TRANSMIT DASHES)	TERMS TABLE	NO. OF MONTH
				5									

PLEASE DO NOT WRITE IN SPACE ABOVE

Direct Mail Order Blank
PLEASE PRINT PLAINLY ONE LETTER IN EACH SPACE

NAME AND PRESENT ADDRESS

NAME (first, middle initial, last) Please use the same name on ALL orders from your household.

SUSAN A LEE

MAILING ADDRESS   APT. NO.

2269 FIRST ST   A-6

CITY/STATE   ZIP CODE

OAKLAND CA   94611

AREA CODE   PHONE NUMBER   TODAY'S DATE

415   925 0830   11 09 81

METHOD OF PAYMENT

☐ Add to my Sears Charge account

My Sears Charge
number is:

My Sears Charge signature: _____

☒ CASH: (check or money order payable to Sears, Roebuck and Co.)

☐ PLEASE OPEN AN ACCOUNT. Completed credit application enclosed.

☐ Amount enclosed to be applied
to my Sears Credit Account $ _____

IF YOUR ADDRESS HAS CHANGED since your last order, please give your old mailing address here:

FORMER ADDRESS   APT. NO. 205

101 S. SHERMAN

CITY/STATE   ZIP CODE

BERKELEY   CA 94704

SHIP TO ANOTHER ADDRESS? If you want this order shipped to another person or to a different address, freight or express station, give address here:

NAME (first, middle initial, last)

MAILING ADDRESS   APT. NO.

CITY/STATE   ZIP CODE

✔ PLEASE GIVE COMPLETE DELIVERY INFORMATION
   Be sure to give complete mailing address at left filling in the correct information, on the lines provided, including telephone number.

✔ PLEASE MAIL ALL INQUIRIES NOT DIRECTLY RELATED TO THIS ORDER UNDER SEPARATE COVER

✔ C.O.D. ORDERS NOT ACCEPTED BY DIRECT MAIL

	CATALOG NUMBER	HOW MANY	COLOR NO. OR SIZE	TOTAL PRICE Dollars	Cents	SHPG. WT. Lbs.	Oz.	Please do not write below Code	Instructions
1	G-836I	1	Size 10	29	99	1	7		
2									
3									
4									
5									
6									
7									

TAX: Please be sure to add correct state, county, city and local taxes applicable.

Fill in spaces below on CASH ORDERS only

	Dollars	Cents		
TOTAL FOR GOODS	29	99	Total Pounds	Total Ounces
TAX (See at left)	1	50	1	7
SHIPPING, HANDLING	3	90	Total Weight in Pounds	
Amount I owe Sears on previous order	—			
TOTAL CASH PRICE	35	39		
AMOUNT ENCLOSED Sears Checks				
Money Order or Check	35	39		

thank you for shopping at Sears

SEARS, ROEBUCK AND CO. *Satisfaction Guaranteed or Your Money Back*

Sears

	DAY	ORDERS	# LINES	SOURCE OF SALE	TYPE SALE	METHOD SHIPMT	CASH	DISCT	TAX EXMT	SPEC CODE	SPECIAL INFORMATION (DO NOT TRANSMIT DASHES)	TERMS TABLE	NO. OF MONTHS
				5									

PLEASE DO NOT WRITE IN SPACE ABOVE

Direct Mail Order Blank
PLEASE PRINT PLAINLY ONE LETTER IN EACH SPACE

NAME AND PRESENT ADDRESS

NAME (first, middle initial, last) Please use the same name on ALL orders from your household.

MAILING ADDRESS   APT. NO.

CITY/STATE   ZIP CODE

AREA CODE   PHONE NUMBER   TODAY'S DATE

METHOD OF PAYMENT

☐ Add to my Sears Charge account

My Sears Charge
number is:

My Sears Charge signature: _____

☐ CASH: (check or money order payable to Sears, Roebuck and Co.)

☐ PLEASE OPEN AN ACCOUNT. Completed credit application enclosed.

☐ Amount enclosed to be applied
to my Sears Credit Account $_____

IF YOUR ADDRESS HAS CHANGED since your last order, please give your old mailing address here:
FORMER ADDRESS APT. NO.

CITY/STATE   ZIPCODE

SHIP TO ANOTHER ADDRESS? If you want this order shipped to another person or to a different address, freight or express station, give address here:
NAME (first, middle initial, last)

MAILING ADDRESS   APT. NO.

CITY/STATE   ZIPCODE

✔ **PLEASE GIVE COMPLETE DELIVERY INFORMATION**
Be sure to give complete mailing address at left filling in the correct information, on the lines provided, including telephone number.

✔ **PLEASE MAIL ALL INQUIRIES NOT DIRECTLY RELATED TO THIS ORDER UNDER SEPARATE COVER**

✔ **C.O.D. ORDERS NOT ACCEPTED BY DIRECT MAIL**

	CATALOG NUMBER	HOW MANY	COLOR NO. OR SIZE	TOTAL PRICE		SHPG. WT.		Please do not write below	
				Dollars	Cents	Lbs.	Oz.	Code	Instructions
1									
2									
3									
4									
5									
6									
7									

TAX: Please be sure to add correct state, county, city and local taxes applicable.

Reprinted courtesy of Sears, Roebuck and Co.

Fill in spaces below on CASH ORDERS only

TOTAL FOR GOODS			Total Pounds	Total Ounces
TAX (See at left)				
SHIPPING, HANDLING			Total Weight in Pounds	
Amount I owe Sears on previous order				
TOTAL CASH PRICE				
AMOUNT ENCLOSED — Sears Checks / Money Order or Check				

thank you for shopping at Sears

2. Here are two sample forms used to apply for a driver's license. The first has been filled in so you can see how to do it. The second is for you to fill in. Use information about yourself.

APPLICATION FOR DRIVERS LICENSE

DRIVERS LICENSE NUMBER		LIC. CLASS	RESTRICTION	EXPIRATION DATE
				MO. ┊ DAY ┊ YR.

FULL NAME

JOSE LUIS GARCIA

RESIDENCE ADDRESS

1628   W. GRACE

CITY OR TOWN	ZIP CODE
CHICAGO	60613

COUNTY	SOCIAL SECURITY NUMBER	HEIGHT FT. ┊ IN.	WEIGHT	COLOR HAIR	COLOR EYES	SEX	DATE OF BIRTH MO. ┊ DAY ┊ YR.
COOK	380 ┊ 26 ┊ 0061	5 ┊ 7	145	BLACK	BROWN	M	6 ┊ 23 ┊ 60

QUESTIONS

1. Is your drivers license or privilege to obtain a license suspended, revoked, cancelled or refused in this or any other state? (If answered "yes," give date, reason, state, etc., below.)   No

2. Is your drivers license being held by a court in lieu of bail? (If answered "yes," explain below.)   No

3. Have you been adjudged to be mentally incompetent and/or been committed to an institution by Court order because of a mental disability? (If answered "yes", a copy of the Order of Restoration and/or a statement from your physician must be presented.)   No

4. Do you have any disability which might cause you to suffer from periods of temporary loss of consciousness? (If answered "yes," a statement will be required from your physician and a medical agreement form must be filed.)   No

5. Do you have any physicial or mental disabilities which could interfere with safe driving (such as heart disease, diabetes, etc.) or do you use any drugs or alcohol to an extent which could impair your driving ability? (If answered "yes", a statement will be required from your physician.)   No

6. Do you have a vision impairment which requires correction to provide adequate vision to drive safely? (If answered "yes," complete the following line.)   YES

Do you wear   glasses ☑   telescopic lenses ☐   contact lenses   Right ☐   Left ☐

EXPLANATIONS: _____

_____

I HEREBY AFFIRM THAT THE INFORMATION I HAVE FURNISHED IN THIS APPLICATION FOR LICENSE IS TRUE TO THE BEST OF MY KNOWLEDGE AND BELIEF.

WRITTEN SIGNATURE OF APPLICANT   _Jose Luis Garcia_

Reprinted courtesy of the State of Illinois, Office of the Secretary of State.

APPLICATION FOR DRIVERS LICENSE

DRIVERS LICENSE NUMBER		LIC. CLASS	RESTRICTION	EXPIRATION DATE		
				MO.	DAY	YR.

FULL NAME

RESIDENCE ADDRESS

| CITY OR TOWN | | | | | | ZIP CODE | | |

COUNTY	SOCIAL SECURITY NUMBER	HEIGHT	WEIGHT	COLOR HAIR	COLOR EYES	SEX	DATE OF BIRTH		
		FT. IN.					MO.	DAY	YR.

QUESTIONS

1. Is your drivers license or privilege to obtain a license suspended, revoked, cancelled or refused in this or any other state? (If answered "yes," give date, reason, state, etc., below.) _____

2. Is your drivers license being held by a court in lieu of bail? (If answered "yes," explain below.) _____

3. Have you been adjudged to be mentally incompetent and/or been committed to an institution by Court order because of a mental disability? (If answered "yes", a copy of the Order of Restoration and/or a statement from your physician must be presented.) _____

4. Do you have any disability which might cause you to suffer from periods of temporary loss of consciousness? (If answered "yes," a statement will be required from your physician and a medical agreement form must be filed.) _____

5. Do you have any physical or mental disabilities which could interfere with safe driving (such as heart disease, diabetes, etc.) or do you use any drugs or alcohol to an extent which could impair your driving ability? (If answered "yes", a statement will be required from your physician.) _____

6. Do you have a vision impairment which requires correction to provide adequate vision to drive safely? (If answered "yes," complete the following line.) _____

Do you wear   glasses ☐   telescopic lenses ☐   contact lenses   Right ☐   Left ☐

EXPLANATIONS: _____

_____

I HEREBY AFFIRM THAT THE INFORMATION I HAVE FURNISHED IN THIS APPLICATION FOR LICENSE IS TRUE TO THE BEST OF MY KNOWLEDGE AND BELIEF.

WRITTEN SIGNATURE
OF APPLICANT _____

3.   Here are two samples of a job application form. The first one has been filled in so you can see how to do it. The second one is for you to fill in. Use information about yourself.

EMPLOYMENT APPLICATION

DATE *5-8-81*

NAME *BROWN   MICHAEL   JAMES*

SOCIAL SECURITY NUMBER *579 -36- 9002*

    LAST   FIRST   MIDDLE

ADDRESS *601 HARVARD ST. N.W. WASHINGTON   D.C.   20005*

    STREET   CITY   STATE   ZIP CODE

PHONE (*202*) *472-8123*

POSITION DESIRED *BINDERY MAN*   DATE YOU CAN START *IMMEDIATELY*   SALARY DESIRED *$6.00/hr.*

Education	NAME AND LOCATION OF SCHOOL	YEARS ATTENDED	DATE GRADUATED	SUBJECTS STUDIED
GRAMMAR SCHOOL	*LASALLE ELEMENTARY SCHOOL WASHINGTON, D.C.*	*1967-1975*	*JUNE, 1975*	*GENERAL*
HIGH SCHOOL	*WILSON HIGH SCHOOL WASHINGTON, D.C.*	*1975-1977*	*—*	*TECHNICAL*
TRADE OR BUSINESS SCHOOL	*UNIVERSITY OF THE DISTRICT OF COLUMBIA WASHINGTON, D.C.*	*1978-1979*	*—*	*PRINTING*

HAVE YOU EVER SERVED IN THE ARMED FORCES? (CIRCLE ONE)   YES   (NO)
(IF YES, GIVE RANK)

            RANK

DO YOU HAVE ANY PHYSICAL LIMITATIONS? (CIRCLE ONE)   YES   (NO)
(IF YES, PLEASE GIVE DETAILS BELOW)

Employment Record (LIST LAST THREE JOBS, STARTING WITH LAST JOB FIRST)

EMPLOYER NAME AND ADDRESS	DATES	POSITION	SALARY	REASON FOR LEAVING
GOODHART PRINTERS, INC. 4110 KANSAS AVE. N.W. WASHINGTON, D.C.	FROM: *5-6-79* TO: *PRESENT*	*BINDERY HELPER*	*$4.50/hr.*	*I WANT TO WORK CLOSER TO HOME.*
THE HAMBURGER HUT 3065 M ST. N.W. WASHINGTON, D.C.	FROM: *6-2-78* TO: *9-3-78*	*BUSBOY*	*$1.00/hr. + tips*	*SUMMER JOB ONLY.*
	FROM: TO:			

References (LIST TWO PEOPLE WHO ARE NOT FAMILY MEMBERS)

NAME	ADDRESS	PHONE	HOW LONG KNOWN
VERONICA GARLAND	*1124 19th ST. N.W.*	*335-4726*	*5 YEARS*
BOBBY LONG	*7206 COLESVILLE RD. SILVER SPRING, MD.*	*251-0774*	*2 YEARS*

BROWN — LAST NAME
MICHAEL — FIRST NAME
JAMES — MIDDLE NAME

EMPLOYMENT APPLICATION

		DATE		
NAME		SOCIAL SECURITY NUMBER - -		
	LAST FIRST MIDDLE			
ADDRESS				
	STREET CITY STATE ZIP CODE			
PHONE ( )				
POSITION DESIRED		DATE YOU CAN START	SALARY DESIRED	

Education	NAME AND LOCATION OF SCHOOL	YEARS ATTENDED	DATE GRADUATED	SUBJECTS STUDIED
GRAMMAR SCHOOL				
HIGH SCHOOL				
TRADE OR BUSINESS SCHOOL				

HAVE YOU EVER SERVED IN THE ARMED FORCES? (CIRCLE ONE)   YES   NO
(IF YES, GIVE RANK)

RANK

DO YOU HAVE ANY PHYSICAL LIMITATIONS? (CIRCLE ONE)   YES   NO
(IF YES, PLEASE GIVE DETAILS BELOW)

(Vertical labels along right edge: LAST NAME / FIRST NAME / MIDDLE NAME)

Employment Record (LIST LAST THREE JOBS, STARTING WITH LAST JOB FIRST)

EMPLOYER NAME AND ADDRESS	DATES	POSITION	SALARY	REASON FOR LEAVING
	FROM:			
	TO:			
	FROM:			
	TO:			
	FROM:			
	TO:			

References (LIST TWO PEOPLE WHO ARE NOT FAMILY MEMBERS)

NAME	ADDRESS	PHONE	HOW LONG KNOWN

4. On the following pages are two samples of a form used in New York to apply for unemployment assistance. Each state has its own form, but these samples are good examples of the kinds of forms government offices often ask you to fill out. The first form has been filled in so you can see how to do it. Fill in the second form with true information about yourself.

NEW YORK STATE DEPARTMENT OF LABOR - Unemployment Insurance Division
ORIGINAL CLAIM FOR BENEFITS
PLEASE PRINT ALL ENTRIES. PRESENT YOUR SOCIAL SECURITY ACCOUNT CARD WITH THIS FORM

1. SOCIAL SECURITY ACCOUNT NUMBER ▶ | 3 | 6 | 3 | 2 | 0 | 8 | 7 | 6 | 4 | DO NOT WRITE IN THE BOX BELOW

2. NAME: FIRST Mary   MIDDLE INITIAL L.   LAST Spright   L.O.

3. ADDRESS: NO.   2296   STREET FLATBUSH AVE.   APT. 601   Date

CITY, TOWN, POST OFFICE BROOKLYN   COUNTY KINGS   ZIP CODE N.Y. 11226   Eff. Date

4a. AGE 27   4b. DATE OF BIRTH MO. 4 DAY 23 YR. 54   5. Show how many people are dependent on you for at least half of their support. (Do not count yourself)
Spouse_____ Children under 18 _1_ Other_____ Total (if none enter zero) _1_

6a. CIRCLE HIGHEST SCHOOL GRADE COMPLETED:
Grade School   High School   College
0 1 2 3 4 5 6 7 8   9 (10) 11 12   13 14 15 16 17+

b. Are you attending school now?   ☐ Yes ☒ No
c. Date last attended if within last year MO. | DAY | YR.

7. What is your present marital status? Check one
☐ Never Married ☐ Married ☒ Divorced ☐ Separated ☐ Widowed

	YES	NO
8. Have you applied for unemployment insurance benefits in this or any other office in this or any other State in the past 52 weeks?	☐	☒

9. Do you expect to go back to work for your last employer? ☒ YES ☐ NO
If "Yes" how soon? _3-4 months_

	YES	NO
10. Was there a strike, lockout or other labor dispute in any place where you worked during the last 8 weeks?	☐	☒

11. Do you belong to a union? If "Yes" enter ☒ Yes ☐ No
name and local. _Amalgamated Clothing Workers_ LOCAL 329

12. Have you applied for or are you receiving:
	YES	NO
a. pension or retirement payment?	☐	☒
b. social security old age or disability retirement benefits?	☐	☒
c. worker's compensation or disability benefits?	☐	☒
d. IRA or KEOGH retirement benefits?	☐	☒

	YES	NO
13. Are you receiving, or will you receive vacation or holiday pay during your present period of unemployment?	☐	☒
14. Do you have any business or are you engaged in any other activity that brings in or may bring in income?	☐	☒
15. In the past 12 months did you work or perform services for a relative, or for a company wholly or partly owned by a relative, or for a partnership or corporation in which a relative is a partner or officer or stockholder?	☐	☒
16. Within the last 12 months have you worked for a corporation of which you were an officer?	☐	☒
17. Did you work under a different name during the last 12 months? If "Yes" what name? _____	☐	☒
18. Are you a citizen of the United States?	☒	☐

19. LIST ALL YOUR EMPLOYERS DURING THE PERIOD FROM   THRU
START WITH YOUR LAST EMPLOYER and work back. Failure to list all your employers and Federal service (civilian and military) may result in a reduced benefit rate or a delay in your benefits. YOUR EMPLOYERS WILL BE NOTIFIED THAT YOU FILED A CLAIM!

DATES	COMPANY NAME OF LAST EMPLOYER COLETTE ORIGINALS
A. BEGAN WORK MO. DAY YR. 6-10-75	ADDRESS 300 STILLWELL AVE.
LAST DAY WORKED MO. DAY YR. 6-1-81	CITY BROOKLYN STATE NY ZIP CODE 11208 CLOCK NO. 30
OCCUPATION ON THIS JOB seamstress

DO NOT WRITE IN ANY OF THE SPACES BELOW.

E.R. NO. ▶

	Weeks	Wages
Total		
Under $40		
Net		
Other		

E
or
C

I AM NOT WORKING FOR MY LAST EMPLOYER BECAUSE:

I was laid off.

IF YOU WORKED FOR ADDITIONAL EMPLOYERS DURING THE ABOVE PERIOD, PLEASE USE THE OTHER SIDE OF THIS FORM. ▶

I hereby register for work and claim unemployment insurance benefits. I certify that I am now unemployed, that I am ready, willing and able to work and that the statements I have made in this application are true and correct. I understand that the law provides severe penalties for wilful false statements to obtain benefits.

LO 330 (10-80)   CLAIMANT SIGN HERE ▶ Mary Spricht

NEW YORK STATE DEPARTMENT OF LABOR - Unemployment Insurance Division
ORIGINAL CLAIM FOR BENEFITS
PLEASE PRINT ALL ENTRIES. PRESENT YOUR SOCIAL SECURITY ACCOUNT CARD WITH THIS FORM

1. SOCIAL SECURITY ACCOUNT NUMBER ▶ | | | | | | | | | | | **DO NOT WRITE IN THE BOX BELOW**

2. NAME: FIRST   MIDDLE INITIAL   LAST   L.O.

3. ADDRESS: NO.   STREET   APT.   Date

   CITY, TOWN, POST OFFICE   COUNTY   ZIP CODE   Eff.
                                      N.Y.   Date

4a. AGE 4b. DATE OF BIRTH   5. Show how many people are dependent on you for at least half of their support. (Do not count yourself)
         MO. DAY YR.
                             Spouse_____ Children under 18 _____Other_____ Total (if none enter zero) _____

6a. CIRCLE HIGHEST SCHOOL GRADE COMPLETED: b. Are you attending school now?   ☐ Yes ☐ No
    Grade School   High School   College
    0 1 2 3 4 5 6 7 8   9 10 11 12   13 14 15 16 17+   c. Date last attended if within last year   MO. DAY YR.

7. What is your present marital status? Check one ☐ Never Married ☐ Married ☐ Divorced ☐ Separated ☐ Widowed

	YES	NO			YES	NO
8. Have you applied for unemployment insurance benefits in this or any other office in this or any other State in the past 52 weeks?	☐	☐	13. Are you receiving, or will you receive vacation or holiday pay during your present period of unemployment?		☐	☐
9. Do you expect to go back to work for your last employer? If "Yes" how soon?_____	☐	☐	14. Do you have any business or are you engaged in any other activity that brings in or may bring in income?		☐	☐
10. Was there a strike, lockout or other labor dispute in any place where you worked during the last 8 weeks?	☐	☐	15. In the past 12 months did you work or perform services for a relative, or for a company wholly or partly owned by a relative, or for a partnership or corporation in which a relative is a partner or officer or stockholder?		☐	☐
11. Do you belong to a union? If "Yes" enter name and local. _____	☐	☐				
12. Have you applied for or are you receiving:			16. Within the last 12 months have you worked for a corporation of which you were an officer?		☐	☐
a. pension or retirement payment?	☐	☐				
b. social security old age or disability retirement benefits?	☐	☐	17. Did you work under a different name during the last 12 months? If "Yes" what name?_____		☐	☐
c. worker's compensation or disability benefits?	☐	☐				
d. IRA or KEOGH retirement benefits?	☐	☐	18. Are you a citizen of the United States?		☐	☐

19. LIST ALL YOUR EMPLOYERS DURING THE PERIOD **FROM**   **THRU**
    START WITH YOUR LAST EMPLOYER **and** work back. Failure to list all your employers and Federal service (civilian and military) may result in a reduced benefit rate or a delay in your benefits. **YOUR EMPLOYERS WILL BE NOTIFIED THAT YOU FILED A CLAIM!**

DATES	COMPANY NAME OF LAST EMPLOYER	*DO NOT WRITE IN ANY OF THE SPACES BELOW.*
A. BEGAN WORK MO. DAY YR.	ADDRESS	
LAST DAY WORKED MO. DAY YR.	CITY STATE ZIP CODE CLOCK **NO.** OCCUPATION ON THIS JOB	*E.R. NO.* ▶				

	Weeks	Wages	
I AM NOT WORKING FOR MY LAST EMPLOYER BECAUSE:	Total			E
	Under $40			or
	Net			C
	Other		

IF YOU WORKED FOR ADDITIONAL EMPLOYERS DURING THE ABOVE PERIOD, PLEASE USE THE OTHER SIDE OF THIS FORM. ▶

I hereby register for work and claim unemployment insurance benefits. I certify that I am now unemployed, that I am ready, willing and able to work and that the statements I have made in this application are true and correct. I understand that the law provides severe penalties for wilful false statements to obtain benefits.

LO 330 (10-80)   **CLAIMANT SIGN HERE** ▶ _____

LETTERS

, Most people need to write letters from time to time. Here's an example of a letter to a child's teacher:

4423 N. Palm St.
Apt. 3
Norveville, AL 29778
May 2, 1981

Dear Mrs. Johnston,
Please excuse my daughter Nancy's absence yesterday. She had a fever of 102° and I thought it best that she stay home in bed.

Very truly yours,
Mrs. Carmen Lopez de Riego

The address in the upper right hand corner belongs to the person who wrote the letter. You should always put your address on your letters so the people who get them can write back to you. Write the date under your address.

Exercise 2

On a separate sheet of paper, write a letter to the phone company. Tell them that they charged you too much on last month's bill. Letters to companies usually begin:

  Gentlemen:
instead of
  Dear So-and-so,

Exercise 3

Write a letter to a friend asking him or her to repay the money you lent last year. Use stationery or a separate piece of writing paper.

PARAGRAPHS

Most writing is divided into paragraphs. Without paragraphs, a newspaper story would look like the one below at left. With paragraphs, it looks like the one at right:

Without Paragraphs	With Paragraphs	
		1st Paragraph
		2nd Paragraph
		3rd Paragraph

As you can see, paragraphs break up the grayness of a long piece of writing. They make the writing easier to read. They make it look more inviting.

Usually each paragraph deals with a different main idea or topic. For example, the following letter has four paragraphs. Each one has to do with a slightly different subject.

Dear Gloria,

Since you left me I have been miserable. I cannot sleep at night. I am too lonely. Nothing means anything to me without you. Food has lost its taste; colors have become black-and-white, and I don't even want to look at other women on the street. I don't even want to watch football on TV anymore.

I admit I was wrong about many things. I did criticize you too much. I didn't look at things from your point of view. I was too selfish. I drank too much. I made you take too much responsibility for things we should have done together. I never remembered to pick up the bath mat after I took a shower.

If you come back, I promise that I'll be different. If you don't come back, I'll never speak to you again.

Love, Fred

As you can see, the first paragraph talks about how Fred has been since his wife left him. The second paragraph lists the things he admits he did wrong. The third paragraph, which is only one sentence long, is a promise. The fourth paragraph is also just one sentence long. It is a threat.

Exercise 4

Use a separate sheet of paper to write a letter to Fred from Gloria which answers the one above. The first paragraph should say why Gloria left him. The second paragraph should say why she does not want to come back. End the letter with one, two, or three other paragraphs.

Exercise 5

Write a letter to someone you admire. In the first paragraph, say how you got to know that person. In the second paragraph, say why you admire him or her. In the third paragraph, wish that person success and luck in the future. You can add more paragraphs on other topics if you wish. Use your own paper.

Exercise 6

Write a letter to your insurance company. In the first paragraph, describe the accident you had with your car. In the second paragraph, say what repairs will be needed and how much they will cost. In the third paragraph, give the names and phone numbers of witnesses who saw the accident. You can add more paragraphs on other topics if you wish. Use a separate piece of paper.

Exercise 7

Write a letter to the building inspector in your city. In the first paragraph, explain that your landlord has not turned on the heat. In the second paragraph, explain that your landlord has not fixed the leak in the kitchen. In the third paragraph, tell how dangerous the exposed wiring in the dining room is. Be sure to describe everything in detail. You can add more paragraphs on other topics if you wish. Use a separate sheet of paper.

MORE ABOUT PARAGRAPHS

By now you probably have a good understanding of paragraphs. Can you figure out the idea behind each paragraph in the following letter?

Dear Mr. Snerd,

I wish to apply for the position of Chairman of the Board of your company. I saw the advertisement you put in the newspaper. I am doing you a big favor by answering because I am exactly the man you are looking for. Let me tell you why.

First of all, I have experience. I am 43 years old and a man learns a lot in 43 years. I've bought a few things from different companies over the years so I know a little bit about them. In particular, your company builds cars, and I know a lot about cars. I've had a driver's license for more than 20 years.

Second of all, I have a few good ideas for your company. General Motors makes good cars, but they are the wrong colors. You should make more cars with dots and stripes and plaids. People want a brighter car. You should also make some with just three wheels and others with five. People get bored with the same old four wheels all the time. I have other ideas, too. I'll be glad to tell them to you some time.

Third of all, I understand that the job pays one million dollars per year. I'll be glad to take the job for just half that, so I'll save you money.

I look forward to hearing from you.

Sincerely yours,

Mr. John Lewis

As you can see, the first paragraph tells why the letter has been written. The second paragraph describes the writer's experience. The third paragraph says that the writer has good ideas. The fourth paragraph talks about money. The fifth paragraph, which is only one sentence long, expresses a wish for the future.

Exercise 8

Write a letter to someone asking for a job. The first paragraph should say why you're writing; the second should describe your experience; the third should describe your ideas about the job; the fourth should talk about money. You can add more paragraphs if you wish. Use a separate sheet of paper.

Exercise 9

Write a letter to the newspaper about a problem in your neighborhood. The first paragraph should describe the problem; the second paragraph should describe what you think should be done about it; the third paragraph should describe what will happen if your solution is not adopted. Add more paragraphs if you wish. Use your own paper.

Exercise 10

Write a letter to the parole board explaining why they should let you out of prison. In the first paragraph, explain how good you've been lately. In the second paragraph, explain why you committed your crime in the first place. In the third paragraph, explain why you would never do it again. In the fourth paragraph, explain how much your family needs you. Use a separate sheet of paper.

AUTOMATIC WRITING

Before a pitcher throws a single ball in a baseball game, he does warm-up exercises. Here's a warm-up exercise for writing. This exercise is easy because however you do it, you can't do it wrong.

Take a piece of paper and a pen or pencil. For five minutes, write down everything that goes through your mind. Everything. Don't stop. Don't worry about spelling, punctuation, or anything else. Just write.

Make up your mind before you start that you won't show your automatic writing to anyone else. This way you will write more freely.

This kind of writing is called automatic writing for the following reason: After you do it for a while, you will see your thoughts coming out on the paper even before you hear them in your head. You will have the feeling that the writing is happening by itself.

Here is a sample of automatic writing. As you can see, mistakes of spelling and grammar don't count in automatic writing:

> Well here goes I've got to write for five
> minutes. What can I say for five minutes?
> Well I guess I can always write my name
> over and over again. Ha-ha. Ha-ha-ha-ha.
> Why am I laughing? That's not funny. This
> is boring. The pen is slippery. I've got other
> things to do. Why am I sitting here doing
> this stupid exercise? Is this really going to
> help me write better? I'm thirsty. I'd like a
> nice cold beer....

5 SPELLING

Spelling may be the hardest thing to learn about English. It may be harder in English than in any other language. But don't worry: there are at least three ways to get good at spelling.

1. Read a lot. Keep a notebook with lists of new words. If you see a word enough times, it will start to look right to you when properly spelled.
2. Study the rules which many words follow.
3. Most important of all: LEARN TO USE A DICTIONARY.

DICTIONARIES

A **dictionary** is just a list of words with some facts about each one. The words are listed in the same order as the letters in the alphabet:

abcdefghijklmnopqrstuvwxyz

Apple comes before **c**arrot in the dictionary, because A comes before C in the alphabet. What if two words have the same first letter? Then the dictionary looks at the <u>second</u> letters: **ne**at comes before **no**te in the dictionary, because E comes before O in the alphabet. What if the first <u>two</u> letters are the same? Look at the third letters: **cot**ton comes before **cou**sin in the dictionary, because T comes before U in the alphabet.

Exercise 1

For each pair of words put a check (✔) next to the word that comes first in the dictionary.

1. quit   ✔
   tuck   ___

2. wing   ___
   deliver   ✔

3. placid   ___
   jurisdiction   ___

4. marry   ___
   ascot   ___

5. foolish   ___
   soon   ___

6. sour   ___
   gravy   ___

Check your answers before going on.

7. wisdom   ___
   folly   ___

8. pretend   ___
   lamp   ___

9. nervous   ___
   null   ___

10. quick   ___
    grave   ___

11. dynamite   ___
    death   ___

12. reckless   ___
    rose   ___

Check your answers before going on.

13. move   ___
    miles   ___

14. arrogant   ___
    archery   ___

15. enough   ___
    eunuch   ___

16. judge   ___
    jeopardy   ___

17. letters   ___
    legume   ___

18. decent ·   ___
    desperate   ___

Check your answers before going on.

19. chap   ___
    char   ___

22. flower   ___
    merchant   ___

20. flatulent   ____   23. bilious   ____
    flattery   ____   venemous   ____

21. vixen   ____   24. wanton   ____
    usufruct   ____   obstruct   ____

Check your answers before going on.

25. taste   ____   28. yes   ____
    nosegay   ____   zebra   ____

26. xylophone   ____   29. broom   ____
    vortex   ____   broomstick ____

27. kiss   ____   30. gadget   ____
    fickle   ____   gasket   ____

Answers start on page 132.

Exercise 2

Here's a list of words in no special order. Write the words on the blanks in alphabetical order, as they would go in a dictionary. As you write them down, cross them off in the left hand column. That way you won't miss any. The first two have been done as examples.

List 1.   sparkle   _____*a*_____
          listen   __*beauty*__
          murder   _____
          foul   _____
          wretched   _____
          ~~beauty~~   _____
          ~~a~~   _____
          the   _____

Check your answers before going on.

List 2. shadow   _____
         mechanic   _____
         underneath   _____
         poetry   _____
         shore   _____
         nefarious   _____
         poem   _____
         bursitis   _____
         ecstasy   _____
         poet   _____

Check your answers before going on.

List 3. phosphorus   _____
         rake   _____
         odious   _____
         toe   _____
         phone   _____
         fix   _____
         rascal   _____
         psychologist   _____
         otiose   _____
         permit   _____
         scissors   _____
         highway   _____

Answers start on page 133.

SPELLING WITH A DICTIONARY

You can always learn how to spell a word by finding it in the dictionary. First imagine the different ways the word might be spelled. Then look up each different way until you find the right one.

For example, suppose you don't know how to spell the word <u>insurance</u>. Make a list of possibilities:

        enshurens
        ensurance
        inshurence
        insurance

And so forth. Look up each possibility. When you find the word in the dictionary, you'll know the right way to spell it.

Exercise 3

WARNING! ALL THESE WORDS ARE SPELLED WRONG!

Write the words correctly in the blanks. If you are not sure how to spell them, use a dictionary. If you have too much trouble finding a word, skip it. The words get harder to find as you go on.

List 1. nise   _____nice_____   crisus   _____
        persun   ____person____   batt   _____
        addres   _____   lok   _____
        rott   _____   mediem   _____

Check your answers before going on.

List 2. folloh   _____   penicilen   _____
        perspirashun   _____   syllibel   _____
        rackit   _____   grievence   _____
        contajus   _____   mickschur   _____

Check your answers before going on.

List 3. labratory   _____   apollogize   _____
        fourman   _____   balence   _____
        liberashun   _____   sannitee

obeedient   _____   cuntagis   _____

Check your answers before going on.

List 4. counterfit   _____   urjent   _____
       manuver   _____   analize   _____
       defendent   _____   absense   _____
       beleeve   _____   hevun   _____

Check your answers before going on.

List 5. prizun   _____   juj   _____
       conveenyent   _____   mekanical   _____
       fashun   _____   hemorrage   _____
       neglijence   _____   frate   _____

Check your answers before going on.

List 6. weerd   _____   collum   _____
       relijus   _____   breckfest   _____
       entrense   _____   orkestruh   _____
       bergler   _____   jewlrey   _____

Check your answers before going on.

These are harder:

List 7. grewsum   _____   fite   _____
       currij   _____   curtesy   _____
       awthur   _____   prejidis   _____
       guvermint   _____   cheef   _____

Check your answers before going on.

List 8. kwick   _____   basickly   _____
       telefone   _____   neese   _____
       gard   _____   familyer   _____
       temprachur   _____   jellus   _____

Check your work before going on.

These are very hard:

List 9. sizzors   _____   sikolojee   _____
         rithem   _____   hipodermick   _____
         fizzishun   _____   chellow   _____
         Artic   _____   greevence   _____

Check your work before going on.

List 10. jepurdize   _____   nawshus   _____
         Febuary   _____   forrin   _____
         newmonya   _____   surjin   _____
         Wensday   _____   offen   _____

Answers start on page 134.

Exercise 4

Get yourself a notebook and write three new words in it everyday. Check the words in a dictionary so you'll know what they mean and how they're spelled. Look back often at all the words you've written. Have someone read your words to you so you can see if you can spell them correctly. If you get into the habit of learning three new words a day, you will become an excellent speller.

VOWELS

Before you can go on, you have to learn about vowels. **Vowels** are these five letters:

a,   e,   i,   o,   u

Sometimes vowels <u>say</u> or sound like their names; sometimes they don't.

Examples:

Hope. The **O** in hope says its name, because hope sounds like **O**.

Hop. The **O** in hop does not say its name.

Sometimes there is more than one vowel:

Feast. The **E** says its name; the **A** is silent.

Head. Neither the **E** nor the **A** says its name.

Exercise 5

Show with a check (✔) whether the vowel says its name. (If there is more than one vowel, does at least one of them say its name?)

List 1.	Says Name	Does Not Say Name		Says Name	Does Not Say Name
sick		✔	fix		
sight	✔		write		
place			cut		
pack			cute		
eat			dope		
get			rock		

Check your answers before going on.

List 2.					
meter			pudgy		
better			useful		
crate			bite		

freight _____ _____   might _____ _____

mute _____ _____   God _____ _____

Check your answers before going on.

List 3.

stuff _____ _____   coat _____ _____

lap _____ _____   heat _____ _____

may _____ _____   eye _____ _____

rough _____ _____   boat _____ _____

feet _____ _____   taste _____ _____

Check your answers before going on.

List 4.

moon _____ _____   great _____ _____

toast _____ _____   crisp _____ _____

grieve _____ _____   pump _____ _____

ache _____ _____   croak _____ _____

Answers start on page 135.

DOUBLING CONSONANTS BEFORE AN ENDING

Once you know the vowels, you are ready for the rule that tells when to double a consonant. **Consonants** are all the other letters which are not vowels. For example, when do you double the consonant P?

tap + ing = taPPing

tape + ing = taPing

When you add ing to tap, you double the **P**. But when you add ing to tape, you don't double the **P**. (Instead you drop the final **E**.) The rule is:

If the vowel says its name, drop the final E (if there is one), but don't double. Otherwise, double.

Examples:

hope + ing = hoping

The **O** in hope says its name, so drop the **E** but don't double.

hop + ing = hopping

The **O** in hop does not say its name, therefore you do double.

This rule applies when adding ing, er, est, ed, and y. Like all rules, this one has plenty of exceptions.

Exercise 6

Add the endings as shown and write the new words on the lines. Remember: If the vowel says its name, drop the final E (if there is one) but don't double. Otherwise, double.

1. rope + ing   *roping*
2. mop + ing   *mopping*
3. read + er   _____
4. red + er   _____

5. fat + er   _____
6. hate + er   _____
7. shake + er   _____
8. wait + er   _____

Check your answers before going on.

9. weak + est   _____
10. bleed + ing   _____
11. sight + ing   _____
12. sit + ing   _____

13. bag + y   _____
14. babe + y   _____
15. cute + er   _____
16. cut + er   _____

Check your answers before going on.

17. date + ed _____   21. leap + ing _____
18. dad + y _____   22. let + ing _____
19. tight + er _____   23. grope + ing _____
20. slip + er _____   24. show + ing _____

Check your answers before going on.

25. rope + ed _____   29. sigh + ing _____
26. hot + er _____   30. knit + ing _____
27. kidnap + er _____   31. bait + ed _____
28. permit + ing _____   32. believe + er _____

Answers start on page 136.

THE I BEFORE E RULE

English has a rule that says when to write **ie** and when to write **ei:**

> I before E
> except after C, and when sounded as A as in
> neighbor or weigh.

In other words, **I** usually goes before **E:**

die

skies

piece

Except after **C:**

receive

ceiling

deceive

And except when sounded as **A:**

sleigh

reign

freight

There are a few exceptions to this rule:

weird	neither	height	conscience
seize	financier	ancient	forfeit
either	foreign	species	leisure

Exercise 7

Some of the following words are misspelled. If a word is spelled wrong, write it correctly on the line. If a word is correct, write "correct."

1. recieve   _receive_   6. sleigh   _____
2. die   _correct_   7. height   _____
3. either   _____   8. peice   _____
4. ceiling   _____   9. decieve   _____
5. neice   _____   10. reign   _____

Check your answers before going on.

11. ancient   _____   16. freind   _____
12. fiend   _____   17. iether   _____
13. height   _____   18. niether   _____
14. wieght   _____   19. neighbor   _____
15. sieve   _____   20. lie   _____

Check your answers before going on.

21. beleive   _____   26. frieght   _____
22. grief   _____   27. peice   _____
23. tie   _____   28. concieve   _____
24. weird   _____   29. wiegh   _____
25. iether   _____   30. consceince   _____

Answers start on page 137.

WORDS WHICH SOUND THE SAME, BUT ARE SPELLED DIFFERENTLY

Be careful with the following words. They sound the same, but have different meanings and different spellings.

gate: door
gait: way of walking

none: not one
nun: woman of God

through: go through
threw: threw a ball

weight: heaviness
wait: pass time

their: belonging to them
there: that place
they're: they are

rain: sky water
reign: king's rule
rein: horse leash

it's: it is
its: belonging to it

weigh: measure heaviness
way: method, direction

know: be aware of
no: opposite of yes

whole: entire
hole: opening

right: correct
write: put on paper

bin: container
been: I've been there

Exercise 8

Some of the underlined words are spelled wrong. If a word is spelled wrong, write it correctly on the line. If a word is spelled correctly, write "correct."

1. I'm dieting because I'm overwait. *overweight*
2. A camel will pass threw the eye of a needle. *through*
3. How many letters did you write? _____
4. Their here. _____
5. They've bin here since Saturday. _____

6. Please close the <u>gate</u>.   _____

7. It's been <u>reining</u> since Saturday.   _____

8. That's the <u>whole</u> story.   _____

9. In your heart you <u>no</u> he's right.   _____

10. Which <u>weigh</u> did he go?   _____

Answers start on page 137.

piece: part
peace: no war

pier: dock
peer: look, equal

too: also
to: toward
two: 2

sleigh: snow vehicle
slay: kill

taut: tight
taught: helped to learn

who's: who is, who has
whose: belonging to
             whom

cell: compartment
sell: give for money

coarse: rough
course: class, path

reed: grass
read: understand book

sew: stitch
so: therefore, thus
sow: plant

red: color
read: I've <u>read</u> the book

sail: part of boat
sale: store event

scene: landscape
seen: I've <u>seen</u> the scene

would: I <u>would</u> if I could
wood: flesh of tree

Exercise 9

Some of the underlined words are spelled wrong. If a word is spelled wrong, write it correctly on the line. If a word is spelled correctly, write "correct."

1. Who <u>taut</u> you to do that?   _____

2. I love to <u>reed</u>.   _____

3. The flag is <u>red</u>, white, and blue.

4. The prisoner was brought to his <u>cell</u>.   _____

5. The little boy went, <u>two</u>.   _____

6. Have you ever <u>seen</u> such a thing?   _____

7. I <u>woodn't</u> do that if I were you.   _____

8. She <u>sowed</u> that dress herself.   _____

9. <u>Who's</u> gloves are these?   _____

10. That <u>peace</u> is too big for me.   _____

Answers start on page 137.

pane: glass	passed: went by
pain: hurt	past: opposite of future
blue: color	weather: rain, snow, sun
blew: pushed air	whether: if
pore: hole in skin	sea: water
pour: spill	see: eye activity
be: to <u>be</u> or not to <u>be</u>	meet: encounter
bee: insect	meat: animal flesh
flue: chimney	site: place
flew: traveled in air	sight: vision
flu: sickness	cite: quote
mane: lion's hair	peek: look
main: most important	peak: point

Exercise 10

Some of the underlined words are spelled wrong. If a word is spelled wrong, write it correctly on the line. If a word is spelled correctly, write "correct."

1. It depends on <u>weather</u> or not you'll be there.   _____

2. I see what you mean.   _____

3. The main thing is not to panic.   _____

4. She'll be 92 in January.   _____

5. She's been sick with the flew for a
    week.   _____

6. They agreed to meat at the restaurant.   _____

7. Don't peak while I'm getting dressed.   _____

8. She pored the rest of it down the
    drain.   _____

9. The child blue out the candles.   _____

10. The rock broke the window pain.   _____

Answers start on page 138.

Exercise 11

Go back to page 128: Words Which Sound the Same but Are Spelled Differently. There are three lists of words. For each set of two or three words, write one sentence. In each sentence use all the words correctly. Use a separate sheet of paper. For instance, the first set was gait and gate. Your sentence might be:

> She noticed his odd gait as he limped through the gate.

For the set their, there, and they're, your sentence might be:

> They're over there near their car.

Check your sentences with a friend.

ANSWERS AND EXPLANATIONS—SPELLING

Exercise 1

1. quit ✔   4. marry
   tuck ___   ascot ✔
                      ✔

2. wing ___   5. foolish ___
   deliver ✔   soon ___

3. placid ___   6. sour
   jurisdiction ✔   gravy ✔

7. wisdom ___   10. quick
   folly ✔   grave ✔

8. pretend ___   11. dynamite ___
   lamp ✔   death ✔

9. nervous ✔   12. reckless ✔
   null ___   rose ___

13. move ___   16. judge ___
    miles ✔   jeopardy ✔

14. arrogant ___   17. letters ✔
    archery ✔   legume ✔
          ✔

15. enough ___   18. decent ___
    eunuch ___   desperate ___

19. chap   ✔
    char   ___

20. flatulent   ___
    flattery   ✔

21. vixen   ___
    usufruct   ✔

22. flower   ✔
    merchant   ___

23. bilious   ✔
    venomous   ___

24. wanton   ___
    obstruct   ✔

25. taste   ___
    nosegay   ✔

26. xylophone   ___
    vortex   ✔

27. kiss   ___
    fickle   ✔

28. yes   ✔
    zebra   ___

29. broom   ✔
    broomstick   ___

30. gadget   ✔
    gasket   ___

Exercise 2

List 1.   a
           beauty
           foul
           listen
           murder
           sparkle
           the
           wretched

List 2.   bursitis
           ecstasy
           mechanic
           nefarious
           poem
           poet
           poetry
           shadow
           shore
           underneath

List 3.   fix   phosphorous
           highway   psychologist
           odious   rake
           otiose   rascal
           permit   scissors
           phone   toe

Exercise 3

List 1.   nice   List 2.   follow
           person   perspiration
           address   racket
           rot   contagious
           crisis   penicillin
           bat   syllable
           lock   grievance
           medium   mixture

List 3.   laboratory   List 4.   counterfeit
           foreman   maneuver
           liberation   defendant
           obedient   believe
           apologize   urgent
           balance   analyze
           sanity   absence
           contagious   heaven

List 5.   prison   List 6.   weird
           convenient   religious
           fashion   entrance
           negligence   burglar
           judge   column
           mechanical   breakfast
           hemorrhage   orchestra
           freight   jewelry

List 7.   gruesome
courage
author
government
fight
courtesy
prejudice
chief

List 8.   quick
telephone
guard
temperature
basically
niece
familiar
jealous

List 9.   scissors
rhythm
physician
Arctic
psychology
hypodermic
cello
grievance

List 10.   jeopardize
February
pneumonia
Wednesday
nauseous
foreign
surgeon
often

Exercise 5

List 1.	Says Name	Does Not Say Name		Says Name	Does Not Say Name
s<u>i</u>ck		✔	f<u>i</u>x		✔
s<u>igh</u>t	✔		wr<u>i</u>te	✔	
pl<u>a</u>ce	✔		c<u>u</u>t		✔
p<u>a</u>ck		✔	c<u>u</u>te	✔	
<u>ea</u>t	✔		d<u>o</u>pe	✔	
g<u>e</u>t		✔	r<u>o</u>ck		✔

List 2.					
m<u>e</u>ter	✔		p<u>u</u>dgy		✔
b<u>e</u>tter		✔	<u>u</u>seful	✔	
cr<u>a</u>te	✔		b<u>i</u>te	✔	
fr<u>ei</u>ght		✔	m<u>i</u>ght	✔	
m<u>u</u>te	✔		G<u>o</u>d		✔

List 3.

st<u>u</u>ff	____	✔	c<u>oa</u>t	✔	____
l<u>a</u>p	____	✔	h<u>ea</u>t	✔	____
m<u>a</u>y	✔	____	<u>e</u>ye	____	✔
r<u>ou</u>gh	____	✔	b<u>oa</u>t	✔	____
f<u>ee</u>t	✔	____	t<u>a</u>ste	✔	____

List 4.

m<u>oo</u>n	____	✔	gr<u>ea</u>t	✔	____
t<u>oa</u>st	✔	____	cr<u>i</u>sp	____	✔
gr<u>ie</u>ve	✔	____	p<u>u</u>mp	____	✔
<u>a</u>che	✔	____	cr<u>oa</u>k	✔	____

Exercise 6

1. roping
2. mopping
3. reader
4. redder
5. fatter
6. hater
7. shaker
8. waiter

9. weakest
10. bleeding
11. sighting
12. sitting
13. baggy
14. baby
15. cuter
16. cutter

17. dated
18. daddy
19. tighter
20. slipper
21. leaping
22. letting
23. groping
24. showing

25. roped
26. hotter
27. kidnapper
28. permitting
29. sighing
30. knitting
31. baited
32. believer

Exercise 7

1. receive	6. correct
2. correct	7. correct
3. correct	8. piece
4. correct	9. deceive
5. niece	10. correct

11. correct	16. friend
12. correct	17. either
13. correct	18. neither
14. weight	19. correct
15. correct	20. correct

21. believe	26. freight
22. correct	27. piece
23. correct	28. conceive
24. correct	29. weigh
25. either	30. conscience

Exercise 8

1. overweight	6. correct
2. through	7. raining
3. correct	8. correct
4. They're	9. know
5. been	10. way

Exercise 9

1. taught	6. correct
2. read	7. wouldn't
3. correct	8. sewed
4. correct	9. Whose
5. too	10. piece

Exercise 10

1. whether   6. meet
2. correct   7. peek
3. correct   8. poured
4. correct   9. blew
5. flu   10. pane

POST-TEST

Directions: The Post-Test gives a final test of the skills you have built. Like the Pre-Test, the 25 questions here test your writing skills in the areas that were covered in this book.

Your skills in these areas should be stronger than they were when you started *Building Basic Skills in Writing, Book 2.*

Follow the directions for each part. There is no time limit, so you may take as long as you need for each question. When you finish, check your answers. Answers and Explanations start at the end of the Post-Test. Fill in the rest of the Test Score Record that you started after the Pre-Test. It is on page 9.

1 MORE ABOUT SENTENCES

These sentences may be poorly written. One of the numbered choices may be better. If so, put a check mark (✔) next to the choice that is better. If no numbered choice is better, check number 5.

1. Carol has a friend what goes to school with us.

_____(1) Carol has a friend which goes to school with us.

_____(2) Carol has a friend who goes to school with us.

_____(3) Carol has a friend and she goes to school with us.

_____(4) Carol has a friend, she goes to school with us.

_____(5) no change

2. Claude found a book that tells how to cook in the bookstore.

_____(1)   Claude found a book which tells how to cook in the bookstore.

_____(2)   A book that tells how to cook Claude found in the bookstore.

_____(3)   Claude found a book in the bookstore, it tells how to cook.

_____(4)   Claude found a book in the bookstore that tells how to cook.

_____(5)   no change

3. While walking down the street, we saw the fire.

_____(1)   We saw the fire walking down the street.

_____(2)   We were walking down the street, we saw the fire.

_____(3)   We saw the fire, we were walking down the street.

_____(4)   While walking down the street and we saw the fire.

_____(5)   no change

4. We talked to a man who went to Peru by telephone.

_____(1)   We talked to a man, he went to Peru by telephone.

_____(2)   We talked by telephone to a man, he went to Peru.

_____(3)   We talked by telephone to a man who went to Peru.

_____(4)   By telephone we talked to a man, he went to Peru.

_____(5)   no change

5. Roses are pretty but have thorns.

_____(1)   Roses are pretty, they have thorns.

_____(2)   Roses are pretty that have thorns.

_____(3)   Roses that are pretty have thorns.

_____(4)   Being pretty, roses also have thorns.

_____(5)   no change

2 PUNCTUATION

One of the underlined punctuation marks may be wrong in each sentence. If so, write its number in the blank. Check number 5 if there is no error.

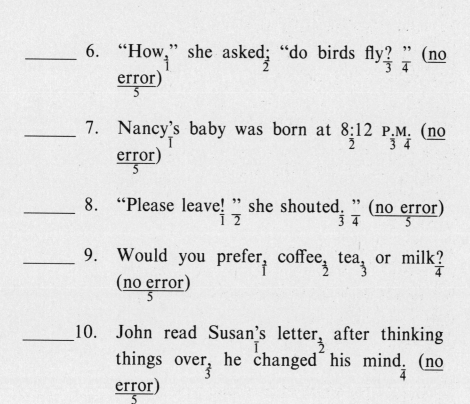

_____ 6.   "How₁," she asked;₂ "do birds fly?₃ "₄ (no error₅)

_____ 7.   Nancy's₁ baby was born at 8:₂12 P.M.₃₄ (no error₅)

_____ 8.   "Please leave!₁ "₂ she shouted.₃ "₄ (no error₅)

_____ 9.   Would you prefer,₁ coffee,₂ tea,₃ or milk?₄ (no error₅)

_____ 10.   John read Susan's₁ letter,₂ after thinking things over,₃ he changed his mind.₄ (no error₅)

3 STYLE

These sentences may be poorly written. One of the numbered choices may be better. If so, put a check mark (✔) next to the choice that is better. If no numbered choice is better, check number 5.

11. The following day after that one she came to a decision
     that she should leave her job.
     _____(1) The next day she decided to quit.
     _____(2) On the very next day she came to the
                conclusion that she ought to quit her job.
     _____(3) She came to a decision that she should
                leave her job the following day after that
                one.
     _____(4) The best thing to do, she decided the next
                day, would be to leave her job.
     _____(5) no change

12. The dog tested the smell in the air with its nose.
     _____(1) With its nose the dog tested the smells in
                the air.
     _____(2) The dog sniffed the air.
     _____(3) Using its sense of smell, the dog inspected
                the air.
     _____(4) The dog checked out the air in terms of
                how it smelled.
     _____(5) no change

13. The giant clam caught the swimmer's leg like glue.
     _____(1) The giant clam caught the swimmer's leg
                like a cold.
     _____(2) The giant clam caught the swimmer's leg
                like a ball.
     _____(3) The giant clam caught the swimmer's leg
                like a bird.
     _____(4) The giant clam caught the swimmer's leg
                like a steel trap.
     _____(5) no change

14. The vault door shut with a clang.
     _____(1) The vault door shut with a loud metallic
                noise.

_____(2)   The vault door shut with a ringing percussive sound.

_____(3)   The vault door shut with a sonic vibration.

_____(4)   The vault door shut with a noise like a clang.

_____(5)   no change

15.   Within seconds after his having hung up, the phone rang another time.

_____(1)   Within seconds after he had hung up the phone rang another time.

_____(2)   Seconds later after he had hung up the phone rang once again.

_____(3)   Seconds had passed after he had hung up the phone and it rang another time.

_____(4)   Seconds after he hung up, the phone rang again.

_____(5)   no change

4 PRACTICAL WRITING

Here is some information about a man. Read the information and use it to fill out this application for a savings account.

The man's name is John Robert Simpson. He was born on March 21, 1925. He lives at 245 West 78th Street in New York City. His zip code is 10021. He lives in Manhattan County. New York City is in New York state. His Social Security number is 160-89-7645. He has brown eyes, brown hair, is 5'10" tall, and weighs 165 lbs. His telephone number is (212) 359-2257.

SAVINGS ACCOUNT—INDIVIDUAL	NEW YORK CITY Savings and Loan

16. ACCOUNT IN NAME OF:_____
                  LAST   FIRST   MIDDLE INITIAL

17. STREET ADDRESS_____

    CITY_____ STATE _____ ZIP CODE _____

18. SOC. SEC. NO._____ TELEPHONE NO. (_____)_____
                                       AREA CODE

PLEASE FILL IN THE FOLLOWING INFORMATION FOR PURPOSES OF IDENTIFICATION ONLY.
(CHECK ONE)
☐ MALE

19. HAIR COLOR _____ EYE COLOR _____ ☐ FEMALE

20. HEIGHT ___|___ WEIGHT _____ BIRTH DATE_____
        FT. IN.   MONTH/DAY/YEAR

5 SPELLING

One word in each group may be misspelled. If a word is misspelled, put a check mark (✔) next to its number. If no word is misspelled, check number 5.

21. _____(1) night
    _____(2) awful
    _____(3) quik
    _____(4) basically
    _____(5) no error

22. _____(1) prison
    _____(2) fashion
    _____(3) judge
    _____(4) burgler
    _____(5) no error

23. _____(1)   telephone
    _____(2)   gaurd
    _____(3)   temperature
    _____(4)   jealous
    _____(5)   no error

24. _____(1)   fierce
    _____(2)   neither
    _____(3)   grievance
    _____(4)   foriegn
    _____(5)   no error

25. _____(1)   weakest
    _____(2)   bleading
    _____(3)   sitting
    _____(4)   baby
    _____(5)   no error

ANSWERS AND EXPLANATIONS—POST-TEST

1 *More About Sentences*

1. (2) Use <u>who</u> or <u>that</u> when adding information about a person.
2. (4) The other sentences makes it seem that Claude is going to cook in the bookstore.
3. (5) no change
4. (3) The other sentences makes it seem that the man traveled by telephone.
5. (5) no change

2 *Punctuation*

6. (2) The semicolon should be a comma.
7. (5) no error
8. (4) There should be no quotation mark here. They are used before and after someone's exact words.
9. (1) Commas here should be used <u>after</u> each item in the series only.
10. (2) This comma should be a semicolon, since both parts of the sentence could be sentences by themselves.

3 *Style*

11. (1) This sentence says it all with the fewest words.
12. (2) This sentence says it all with the fewest words.
13. (4) This sentence says it all with the fewest words.
14. (5) no change
15. (4) This sentence says it all with the fewest words.

4 *Practical Writing*

SAVINGS ACCOUNT—INDIVIDUAL	NEW YORK CITY Savings and Loan

16. ACCOUNT IN NAME OF: *Singerson   John   R.*
    LAST   FIRST   MIDDLE INITIAL

17. STREET ADDRESS *245 West 78th Street*
    CITY *New York City* STATE *New York* ZIP CODE *10021*

18. SOC. SEC. NO. *160-89-7645* TELEPHONE NO. (*212*) *359-2257*
    AREA CODE

PLEASE FILL IN THE FOLLOWING INFORMATION FOR PURPOSES OF IDENTIFICATION ONLY.

(CHECK ONE)

☑ MALE

19. HAIR COLOR *brown* EYE COLOR *brown* ☐ FEMALE

20. HEIGHT *5* | *10* WEIGHT *165* BIRTH DATE *Mar. 21 1925*
    FT.   IN.   MONTH/DAY/YEAR

5 *Spelling*

21. (3) <u>quick</u> is the correct spelling.
22. (4) <u>burglar</u> is the correct spelling.
23. (2) <u>guard</u> is the correct spelling.
24. (4) <u>foreign</u> is the correct spelling.
25. (2) <u>bleeding</u> is the correct spelling.